You Are
the Splendor

The Way to Spiritual
Illumination

Writings by Marie S. Watts

These and other books by Marie S. Watts
are available through:
Mystics of the World
Eliot, Maine
www.mysticsoftheworld.com

You Are
the Splendor

The Way to Spiritual
Illumination

Marie S. Watts

You Are the Splendor

Mystics of the World First Edition 2015
Published by Mystics of the World
ISBN-13:978-0692432907
ISBN-10:0692432906

For information contact:
Mystics of the World
Eliot, Maine
www.mysticsoftheworld.com

Cover graphics by Margra Muirhead
Printed by CreateSpace
Available from Mystics of the World and Amazon.com

Marie S. Watts

Originally published 1966

I Am the One

I am the only One, the All,
I am the One 'pon whom I call
when darkness doth appear,
or when I seem to fear
some presence, power, or blight
that could obscure the Light.

I am the heaven and the earth;
I am the Life that knows no birth,
no change, no age, no death.

I am the One, the only Mind,
the One it seemed that I must find,
till I awoke to see
the I AM that is ME.

To You the Reader

You will discover that the truths presented within these pages are already included in and as your own Consciousness. A contemplative study of this book will serve as a reminder of the basic truths you know, but seem to have forgotten.

Note to the Reader

For consistency of interpretation, the following words almost always have a capital letter initial because each one stands for God or God's identification of Itself as the attribute for which the word stands:

Almighty	Omniaction
Body of Light	Omnipotence
Consciousness	Omnipresence
Earth planet	Perfection
Essence	Principle
Identity	Reality
Intelligence	Soul
Life	Spirit
Light	Substance
Love	Truth
Mind	Universe

Other words are capitalized when they are used as a synonym *for* God but not as a descriptive activity or attribute *of* God:

Absolute	Immensity
Activity	Immutability
Actuality	Infinite, the
All, Allness	Infinitude
Awareness	Infinity
Beauty	Itself
Being	Joy
Body	Known, the
Completeness	Nature
Ear	One, Oneness
Entirety	Onliness
Eternity, Eternality	Peace
Everything	Presence
Everywhere, the	Radiance
Existence	Self
Existent	Sense
Experience	Something
Eye	Supply
Hearing	Totality
Heart	Vision
I	Wholeness

Contents

Introduction

Always, whenever a need seems great enough, the Truth that is necessary at the moment appears. Today the world seems to be in the greatest trouble it has ever known. And mankind itself seems to be beset by continuously increasing mental and physical difficulties. All efforts by human organizations have failed to solve the self-made problems of the world, and all efforts of the human mind have failed to solve the self-made problems of mankind, or to arrest the appearance of new types of problems. Laudable as all these efforts may be, they cannot succeed because they are being made from the level of the problem. In other words, it is the assumptive human mind which is the basic reason for all the problems, and the mind that engenders and prolongs the problems is incapable of solving them. Something greater than the assumptive human mind must be realized if the apparent problems of the world and of mankind are to be obliterated. This "Something" is *illumined Consciousness.*

The specific purpose in the presentation of this book is the *illumination,* or enlightenment, of everyone who reads and contemplates the truths herein presented. If it is possible for this purpose to be fulfilled — and it is — the world as well as the individual will be enlightened. Thus, the peoples of the world will enjoy greater freedom, health, peace, and joy. The world is constituted of individuals; thus, the truths perceived and evidenced by the individual must benefit the entire world.

There is no way to estimate the tremendous power of one enlightened individual. As the number of these illumined individuals increases, so it is that the entire world becomes more enlightened. An enlightened individual is a healthy, joyous, free individual. An enlightened world would necessarily be a harmonious, joyous, peaceful, and free world.

Illumined Consciousness is the answer to the problems of the world and its people. But if illumined Consciousness is to be realized, it is necessary to know what It is, what It means, and how It functions for the benefit of the identity and the world. This book differs sharply from the commonly accepted theory that illumination is the prerogative of but a few chosen ones. It reveals that there is nothing mysterious or supernatural about enlightened Consciousness. It takes all the mystery out of this perfectly normal experience and shows the way in which the individual can discover illumined Consciousness to be his own Consciousness.

A contemplative study of this book will acquaint the reader with an aspect of his own Consciousness that he may not have realized heretofore. All revelation is necessarily self-revelation, and revelation of the Self reveals the splendor of the limitless Consciousness which *is* the normal Mind of every individual. A normal Mind engenders health, peace, and happiness for the individual as well as for the world. In other words, this book is a means of Self-discovery, and in this discovery the Self that seems to have been hidden is revealed.

You Are the Splendor ...

Takes the mystery out of illumination;
Reveals the way to experience illumination;
Reveals the way illumination solves problems.

Chapter I

Illumination

In him was life; and the life was the light of men.
—John 1:4

Much has been spoken and written about illumination. Yet there seems to be little understanding of the true meaning of this word. There are some who avoid the use of the word *illumination* because it has, to them, a mysterious or supernatural connotation. Actually, there is nothing mysterious or supernatural about the experience of illumination. On the contrary, this experience is perfectly natural and normal. Furthermore, it is possible to live as illumined beings. It is possible to walk, talk, and carry on our daily affairs as illumined ones. Those who have realized this fact discover that they are living normal lives in every way—the only difference being that the struggle, the strain, and the worry are completely eliminated. Needless to say, there is no more fear, sadness, or grief.

An illumined being is a happy, busy, normal individual. An illumined being is an identity who lives, loves, and acts impersonally, in freedom, in strength, and in joyous peace. There are many such individuals walking the earth today, in freedom and in joy.

17

Let *us* perceive just what it means to be an illumined being. Our first step in this realization must be the obliteration of all false sense that illumination is a mysterious or supernatural experience. Heretofore, it has been widely believed that illumination could only be experienced by a small, select group. These favored ones were considered to be particularly gifted with spiritual insight and were given the title of master, leader, guru, or some other title which set them apart from — and placed them above — their students and followers. It is true that spiritual insight is requisite for illumination. But this does not mean that only a chosen few are endowed with the faculty of spiritual perception.

Actually, there is no one living who is completely devoid of spiritual perception. Spiritual perception really means *Spirit perceiving*. Perception must be an activity of Consciousness, and it follows that spiritual perception is Consciousness actively perceiving. Enlightened Consciousness is Spirit.

Of course, when we speak of enlightened Consciousness being Spirit, we are not referring to a human consciousness. That which is called the human consciousness can never be or become spiritually perceptive. The things of Spirit are only perceived by the Consciousness that is Spirit. Job was aware of this fact when he said, "But there is a spirit in man: and the inspiration of the Almighty giveth them understanding" (Job 32:8). John also perceived this truth, and he made it clear that every

18

Identity in existence is imbued with this spiritual awareness. "That was the true light, which lighteth every man that cometh into the world" (John 1:9).

You will note that John speaks of the Light as the *true* Light. The *true* Light is the genuine Light. The genuine Light is spiritually enlightened Consciousness. The genuine Consciousness of every Identity that "cometh into the world" is enlightened Consciousness. Enlightened Consciousness is illumined Consciousness, and illumined Consciousness is the Consciousness of an Identity who perceives the "things of Spirit" with the spiritual vision that *is* illumination.

It is true that some of us appear to be more aware of "seeing" spiritually than are others. Yet the fact remains that each and every Identity has the capacity to see with the eye of Spirit. By this we mean that every Identity is imbued with the enlightened Consciousness which is capable of spiritual perception, or illumination.

The word *faculty* is often used to denote the visual, the aural, or one of the other five senses of man. Yet there is a much greater and more satisfying concept of this word. Shakespeare has said, "What a piece of work is a man! how noble in reason! how infinite in faculty." Certain it is that this use of the word *faculty* means more than a human faculty called vision, hearing, etc.

The word *faculty*, when understood in this larger sense, may be used to denote the illumined

Consciousness which is a faculty of every Identity in existence. Throughout the ages, there have been those who were aware of the endowment of this faculty. Lao-tzu, the great Chinese illumined one, was called a mystic. Yet he claimed no such title or distinction for himself. Beyond doubt, he was one of the greatest, if not *the* greatest, of all illumined ones.

Another one of tremendous spiritual insight was Shankara. Then, of course, there was the great Buddha, our own beloved Jesus, the Christ, and numerous others. Our own Bible records many cases of illumined Consciousness. Abraham, Jeremiah, Isaiah experienced moments of tremendous illumination. David, the psalmist, was certainly illumined. He must have experienced being illumined Consciousness as he watched over the sheep under the limitless skies. This is obvious from many of the Psalms.

At least one illumined episode is recorded of the disciples of Jesus. It is recorded that Jesus took Peter, James, and John, his brother, to a high mountain "and was transfigured before them: and his face did shine as the sun, and his raiment was white as the light" (Matt. 17:2). Here is a definite description of that which takes place when illumined Consciousness perceives the genuine being and body of *anyone*. One such incident as this should convince us that enlightened Consciousness is not an exclusive endowment of but a few individuals.

The next important fact to be recognized is that illumination, or enlightened Consciousness, is perfectly natural. It is a *normal* experience. And when we arrive at the point of living as an illumined being, we realize that this is the *only* normal way to live.

As stated before, illumined Consciousness is an innate faculty of each and every individual. Furthermore, illumined Consciousness is frequently experienced by everyone, in one way or another. We have biblical authority for the foregoing statement. "In him was life; and the life was the light of men" (John 1:4). This is an absolute Truth. The Life *is* the Light of men. But we must realize that Light is the *Life* of men also. Without Life, there would be no Light. Conversely, without Light, there would be no Life. To be alive is to be alight. To be alight is to be alive.

Now let us perceive how it is that often we experience illumination, although, at the moment, we may not recognize it as such. For instance, everyone has had the experience of realizing the knowledge of some fact without having been taught this fact. Furthermore, he knows that he has not heard it, read it, or in any way learned it. He cannot humanly explain just how it is that he knows this fact, but he knows it beyond any doubt. Illumined Consciousness is the *only* Consciousness that can know any fact without the aid of some human agency.

The innate knowledge of certain facts exists within and as the Consciousness of every one of us.

This is noticeably apparent in the case of prodigies. A prodigy is simply one whose Consciousness is illumined in some specific aspect. This illumination may pertain to music, to mathematics, to art, or to innumerable other aspects of existence. Just as there are innumerable aspects of existence, so it is that there are innumerable aspects of illumination.

As the student perceives and understands the various aspects of illumination, he will also recognize the fact that his own Consciousness is already enlightened Consciousness. This eradicates all the mystery and supernaturalness attached to the word *illumination*, and the student can approach greater illumination with more confidence and without any feeling that he is unworthy or inadequate to have this glorious experience. It also gives him a basis from which to start, and his approach will be made with more freedom and expectancy. Most important of all is the fact that illumination will now be perceived as a perfectly normal experience; thus he can live a perfectly balanced and normal existence as an illumined being.

Chapter II

Aspects of Illumination

As stated in the preceding chapter, there are innumerable aspects of illumination. In addition to this, there are various *degrees* of the awareness of illumination. Let us now explore some aspects of this experience and begin to understand just how complete is any illumined experience.

Illumination may be experienced visually or aurally. It may be evident as a delightful sense of perfume. Again, it may be a bodily experience. This experience may appear as a wonderful tingling sense throughout the entire body. It may be compared to a vibrant but gentle electric sense, as if the body were charged with electricity. Again, it may be just a warm flow of peace and love throughout the body.

Illumination may be just knowledge of some fact without having acquired this knowledge in any way. Again, it may be a sudden awareness of some act that must be performed immediately. Perhaps a letter must be written, a call made, or it may be that a trip must be taken. Again, this is an inner knowledge which cannot be explained from the standpoint of the human experience.

In some moments of illumination there is a sense of being weightless. Not only is the body without weight but there is an awareness that the floor has neither solidity, density, nor weight.

Now let us explore, in greater detail, some of these illumined experiences. Let us begin with the aural aspect of illumination. All of us have heard of "the music of the spheres." In fact, Guy Murchie, a well-known writer, has written a wonderful book entitled *Music of the Spheres.* Mr. Murchie does not claim to be a metaphysician or a mystic. In his approach, we find a blending of literature, philosophy, and science into one universal, harmonious whole. There can be no doubt but that he has heard the music of the spheres. One such instance as this is proof that it is possible for *anyone* to have this experience. Herein is the primary fact revealed:

Illumination is not just the prerogative of those who call themselves mystics or metaphysicians.

There are many individuals who have heard the music of the spheres. It is noteworthy that many of these individuals made no claim to exceptional spiritual insight. In fact, some of them would scoff at the very suggestion that there *was* such a thing as illumined Consciousness. Yet the fact remains: they *did* experience aural illumination. Only an illumined Consciousness can hear this divine music.

We mention the aspect of aural illumination first because this is the most frequently reported experience of this kind. No human instruments or voices could possibly reproduce this music. It is beyond description. In fact, it must be heard if one is to know and experience its beauty. In the most complete awareness of this aspect of illumination, one has the feeling of actually *being* the music one is hearing.

Sometimes the music of the spheres may be heard as if it were the singing of innumerable birds. It is so beautifully blended that the song of no one bird is distinguishable from another. Yet there is a joyous, surging, rhythmic, tonal, audible harmony. Furthermore, one knows that one is actually *hearing* this music and that it is no hallucination.

Music of the spheres may be heard as if it were being played by an infinite symphony orchestra, comprising innumerable instruments having no earthly counterpart. Here again, the music is so beautifully merged that it would be impossible to distinguish one instrument from another. One also hears the same surging, joyous, rhythmic harmony that is heard when the birdlike music is audible.

Of course, all of us love good music and the joyous songs of birds. However, right here it must be noted that it is impossible to compare *any* earthly music with the music of the spheres. For one thing, there are no earthly birds that could produce this glorious, divine music. Furthermore, there are no orchestral instruments that could possibly reproduce the delicate, yet intense, tones and harmonies one hears as this heavenly music.

After having heard the heavenly music, one would expect that any earthly music would appear gross and coarse. In one way, this is true. But paradoxically, more often than not our enjoyment of good music—whether of birds or of orchestral instruments—is greatly enhanced through having heard the indescribably beautiful music of the spheres. We seem to sense the more glorious music, even as we are listening to concerts or to the songs of birds. I have found this to be particularly true when I have heard the music of Bach being exceptionally well performed. The music of Bach has been said to be the most spiritual of all music. This may account for my experience of great illumination when hearing his music beautifully played.

It is essential that we diverge for a moment here because there is an important point that must be clarified. We have mentioned various aspects of illumination. We have discussed, to some extent, aural illumination. This does not mean, however, that there is a genuine separation *between* various aspects of illumination. It is Consciousness that sees, that hears, and that experiences. The Consciousness that sees also hears and experiences. Consciousness is not divided, although Consciousness may be aware of various distinct aspects of Its awareness. We get a hint of this fact when we realize that we may see, hear, and experience simultaneously. The indivisibility of Consciousness will be thoroughly revealed during the succeeding chapters of this work.

There have been reports of aural illumination experienced in ways other than those mentioned here. However, the foregoing aspects of this experience are sufficient for our purpose. Anyone experiencing aural illumination of *any* nature should now recognize and understand just what is taking place.

Let us now turn our attention to another aspect of illumination. There are events of illumined Consciousness that can be described only as an *experience*. For instance, one may be in a room, with all the doors and windows closed, and suddenly one will feel a soft, gentle breeze wafting across his face. This is one of the most frequent experiences of illumination.

Sometimes, for no apparent reason, a wonderful sense of peace will permeate the entire being. This sense of peace is beyond any human understanding or explanation. It is so complete that the entire body suddenly experiences a warm glow of ineffable peace. Often this glorious sense of peace will suddenly be realized when one seems to be greatly disturbed or even in bodily pain. It is an assurance that all is well, despite all appearances to the contrary. And generally, this subsequently proves to be true. It is noteworthy that more often than not this infinite sense of peace presages the *full* realization that all *is* well. Furthermore, this realization is evidenced as that which is called healing.

It is obvious that the foregoing experience can only take place in and *as* illumined Consciousness. The assumptive, reasoning, human mind could never be aware of such peace when one seemed to be in the very midst of great trouble or pain. Illumined Consciousness may be compared to the sun, which is always present but may temporarily be obscured by very dark clouds. Sometimes there will suddenly be a rift in the clouds, and the glorious sun will show forth in all its splendor. Thus it is that enlightened Consciousness may suddenly burst through the seeming barrier, and omnipresent Perfection may be realized and evidenced.

Another aspect of illumination is joy. Suddenly an inexplicable sense of joy will flood the entire Consciousness. This illumined event may transpire when one is in deep contemplation; or it may instantaneously be manifested at any moment of the day or night. It is an ecstatic, vital, living sense of joy which cannot be accounted for or explained from any human standpoint. It is sheer joy, without any human reason for being particularly joyous. It far transcends any experience that could be termed human happiness or enjoyment. The ecstasy of this illumination may be experienced even when you are seemingly troubled or in pain. Obviously, then, this is illumination because from the standpoint of human reasoning, it simply could not take place under such circumstances.

It often happens that this illumination may be evidenced just prior to the obliteration of some seeming problem. From this it is evident that illumined Consciousness simply reveals the Perfection that *does* exist rather than the imperfection which does not exist. Actually, all phantasmic sense of inharmony is obliterated when you are experiencing illumined Consciousness. This is true whether the predominating factor of the illumination appears as peace, joy, an illumined experience, or whatever.

From this it should be clear that illumination reveals the genuine and *only* nature of Existence. Once the eternal, immutable Perfection which does exist is perceived, any distorted misconception *about* genuine Existence is obliterated. Then you will probably say that you have had a healing. But deeper perception reveals that no healing has actually taken place. Rather it is that omnipresent Perfection has been so clearly realized that the fallacious appearance of illness or trouble is simply canceled out.

This explains just why it is so necessary to consciously experience illumination—and to recognize the true nature of this experience. In fact, this is one reason why this book has been written.

Among the various phases of illumination is one outstanding experience that must be mentioned here. This experience is particularly difficult to describe in words, as there are so many ramifications of the one experience. Nevertheless, we shall attempt to portray this aspect of illumination. It is important that you understand this type of experience for the following reason: *so often it engenders much fear.* Many of you have experienced the following phase of illumination and, because you have not understood it, have been very frightened. Some of you are even loath to talk about it.

Now let us calmly and intelligently investigate the illumination in which all solidity and density disappear, yet you are aware that you exist and that your existence includes a body. However, you discover that you are not confined to the body or even to its immediate vicinity.

You may suddenly feel that you are standing just behind the body, but the body has no solidity. You may be seeing the body from across the room or even from the ceiling. Again, you may suddenly discover that you are in another city entirely. You may be walking around, fully comprehending all the various elements that constitute that city. You may be aware of the body; but again, you may have no awareness of body at all. In the latter event, it is just a matter of *being* in that specific city. One outstanding fact pertaining to this event is that you have no awareness of having projected yourself anywhere. You have no sense of going anywhere. Suddenly you are *there.*

There is much greater illumination of your timeless, spaceless nature, but we will not discuss this just now. For the time being, let us just say that you have discovered the limitless freedom that is inherently your divine Nature.

Please be assured that there is nothing to fear in this phase of illumination. It happens frequently, and it has been the experience of innumerable individuals throughout the ages. It is only recently that we have begun to realize that this is a perfectly normal experience. Jesus was well aware of the normality of this event. You will remember that the windows and doors were closed when he suddenly appeared in the room with the disciples. Then, too, we have biblical authority for the fact that Jesus saw Nathanael, although from any human standpoint they seemed separated by such distance that this would have been impossible. You will find this episode recorded in John 1:43-50.

There are also many recent authenticated incidents of this kind, and they are becoming more numerous all the while. We will not pursue this line of inquiry any further just now. But please be assured that there is nothing mysterious or supernatural about this aspect of illumined experiences.

There is a perfectly logical explanation for these occurrences. When illumination is understood, all false sense of mystery or mysticism is abolished. This leaves you free to *let* these illumined experiences perform the glorious works which is the purpose of their appearing.

As you continue your study and contemplation of this book, *you* will perceive the nature of illumination, and you will discover the pure, logical Intelligence of this experience. Furthermore, you will also realize the glorious freedom and perfection that naturally accompanies being an illumined individual.

Chapter III

Spiritual Perception

The subject of vision is of vital importance to all seekers along the spiritual path. This is true because our judgment of Existence depends primarily upon that which we see. It is quite well known that the vision of man is incapable of reporting correctly what it seems to see. This knowledge is not confined to just those of us who are "seeing" spiritually. Any physicist will readily admit that things are not as they appear to be when seen by the eye of man.

Sir Arthur Eddington is acknowledged to be one of the greatest of many renowned physicists. In one of his later works, he makes it very clear that we do not see substance as it genuinely is. His inference is that between the seeing of an object and the object itself something happens which changes its appearance. Of course, in this instance he is referring to matter. But *matter* is such an overworked and misunderstood word that I prefer the words *density* or *solidity*.

Anyone who is aware of being illumined would thoroughly agree with Sir Arthur Eddington. It is true that Existence cannot be seen as It is when the vision seems to be filtered through the veil called the eye of man. You see, the eye believes what it sees.

That which is called the eye of man consists of an illusionary substance. That which it seems to see and report is also constituted of illusion. The illusionary substance called the eye and the supposititious substance called the object which it sees are exactly the same illusion. The meaning of this statement may seem obscure at the moment, but it will be clarified as you continue in this book.

If you were unconscious, you would see nothing at all. This would be true even if your eyes were wide open. Therefore, it is obvious that the eye, of itself, sees nothing and can report nothing. Thus, we arrive at the conclusion that the eye itself is not what it appears to be. From a human standpoint, there is still much mystery concerning the eye. It will continue to be a mystery until the true nature of all Substance is perceived, and this can be realized only as Consciousness is illumined.

The following statement may seem completely unreasonable to you just now, but if you continue reading, you will perceive that it is entirely reasonable. More important, it is true.

Illumined Consciousness sees equally well, whether or not the eyes are open. Illumined Consciousness sees everything that is in the range of so-called human vision. It sees much more than is visible to the veil called a human eye, and above all, It sees things *as they are.*

Neither the eye nor the eyelid can obstruct or confine spiritual Vision. Illumined Consciousness is spiritual Vision, and spiritual Vision is Spirit, or Soul, or Consciousness "seeing."

We are well acquainted with the word *Spirit*. Yet this word has very little genuine meaning for most of us. Generally, it denotes something intangible, nebulous, without essence, form, or activity. Perhaps one has a more definite concept of the word *Soul*. This is true because the Soul is supposed to have an identity, and It is presumably identified with a body.

There is one word which encompasses the meaning of these two words Spirit and Soul; it brings into intelligent focus their significance. This word is *Consciousness*. There is no word in our language that is so fraught with spiritual significance as is the word *Consciousness*. Spirit, Soul, Consciousness have exactly the same meaning. They may be used interchangeably, but the meaning remains the same. So let us dwell with this word *Consciousness* for a while and discover, at least to some extent, the genuine Essence and activity of that which we call *Consciousness*.

Consciousness is awareness. To be conscious is to be aware. To be unconscious would mean to be unaware. You are aware that you exist. If you were not conscious, you would *not* be aware that you exist. So Consciousness is awareness of Existence.

We have just stated that Consciousness, Spirit, and Soul are identical. Thus, Spirit is your own awareness that you exist. Soul is likewise this same awareness. *Spiritual Consciousness is illumined Consciousness.* It will not be difficult for you to perceive that Soul is spiritual. On the contrary, it will be simple for you to realize that Soul, being conscious, is spiritual Consciousness. Thus, it should be clear that illumined Consciousness is the Soul you *are*, being aware of Existence as It is.

There is another expression used to denote illumined Consciousness. Sometimes we hear or read the words *Cosmic Consciousness*. This is a much misunderstood expression. It is often used with a connotation of mysticism, as if it were something supernatural. The word *cosmic* pertains to the Cosmos. Webster defines the word *cosmos* as "the universe as an orderly and harmonious system," as contrasted with chaos. Cosmic Consciousness is universal Consciousness. It is the universal awareness of perfect order and complete harmony. Thus, Cosmic Consciousness is *conscious* of being order, perfection, and harmony.

Spiritual Consciousness is Cosmic Consciousness. This means that Cosmic Consciousness is illumined Consciousness. It is illumined, or enlightened, universal Awareness. Cosmic Consciousness is an awareness of the infinitude we call the Universe. It is illimitable, and It cannot be contained or confined. Certain it is that universal Consciousness cannot be limited to just one little area; much less can it be imprisoned within the bounds of time and space. It has no awareness of boundaries of any nature. It is indivisible. It is immeasurable in terms of fallacious time and space.

This is the Consciousness that is illumined. This is enlightened Consciousness. This is the *only* genuine Consciousness in existence. Thus It is the Consciousness that you are, and It is the Consciousness that I am. The pseudo mind of man is *not* this glorious, free, boundless, limitless Consciousness.

Just as surely as there is a Soul, there is illumined Consciousness. It is impossible to conceive of Soul as being mortal or material. No one denies that he has a Soul. Why, then, should anyone deny that he has an illumined Consciousness? Before you have finished with this book, you will discover not only that you *have* a Soul, or an illumined Consciousness; but that you *are* Soul. You *are* illumined Consciousness.

At the beginning of this chapter we stated that we do not see things as they really are. Now let us begin to perceive just why our vision apparently reports such distorted pictures.

Earlier in this chapter, we mentioned the fact that Existence cannot be correctly seen when viewed through the *veil* called the eyes of man. There are many references in our Bible pertaining to the veil which seems to cloud our vision. "And he will destroy in this mountain the face of the covering cast over all people, and the veil that is spread over all nations" (Isa. 25:7).

The great prophet Isaiah must have had many illumined experiences. Many of his statements are pure, absolute Truth. You will note his perception that *all people* and *all nations* appear to be victimized by this veil that obscures the true and only Existence. Only an illumined Consciousness could have been aware that the veil only *seemed* to cast a shadow over that which is genuine. Furthermore, he realized that this "covering" would be obliterated. Isaiah was seeing things as they *are,* and he knew that ultimately everyone must be aware of Existence as It is.

A veil could be referred to as something which is interposed between the vision and that which is seen. This would mean that a separation exists *between* the seer and that which is seen. Thus, there would have to be an assumption of twoness, or dualism. Now we have arrived at the key word of all our seeming difficulty: *dualism.* In Webster's unabridged dictionary we find the following definition:

> *Dualism* A twofold division; any theory which considers the ultimate nature of the universe to be twofold, or to be constituted by two mutually irreducible elements.

Dualism is division. It inevitably presents an illusory picture of separateness between the one who sees and that which is seen. This is the veil spoken about in the Bible. In my book entitled *The Ultimate,* there is a chapter with the title "Seeing Is Being." I will not repeat the Truth revealed in *The Ultimate,* but it would be helpful to read and correlate that chapter with what you are now reading.

Now let us perceive just what it is that seems to separate the seer from that which is seen. Let us also perceive the reason why that which is seen *appears* to be distorted.

It is the false concept called a human eye that appears to separate the one who is seeing from that which is seen. It is the fallacy that vision must be filtered through these same eyes of man that presents a distorted picture of that which is seen.

We have said that if one were unconscious, one would see nothing. This is proof positive that the eye does *not* see. Vision is perception. Perception is an activity of Consciousness. So vision is Consciousness perceiving. In other words, vision is an activity of Consciousness.

It is impossible for the eyes of man to see things as they are. That which we call man is but an illusion *about* the eternal Identity. Any illusion must be an illusion about something that does exist. The Identity does exist. The illusion *about* the Identity does not exist. It has no identity, no substance, form, or activity.

The illusion called the body of man is but one aspect of innumerable illusions. These innumerable illusions are but aspects of a universal illusion. An illusion can *appear* genuine only to one who is deluded by it. This one would have to be man with "breath in his nostrils." But the Bible makes it clear that we are to "cease ye from man, whose breath is in his nostrils: for wherein is he to be accounted of?" (Isa. 2:22).

There is no accounting for man with breath in his nostrils. If God be All—and God *is* All—then this temporary assumptive man is non-existent. The eternal Life which is God cannot live as a temporal life. Thus, there is no such life. Yet this assumptive man does appear to be born, to live temporarily, and to die.

This is the illusion. All that pertains to human birth, human life, and human death is illusion. The very deluded one called a human being is an illusion. The assumptive mind and body of this illusion *must* consist of the illusion itself; thus, it would have to be the deluded one. Here we have the fact:

> The deluded one is the illusion itself. Neither the illusion nor the deluded one has existence.

Assumptive man—the deluded one—and *any* illusion are the same thing: illusion. Assumptive man can see *only* his own illusions. A so-called deluded one, seeing its own illusions, is intrinsically illusory. It is a phantasmic delusion *about* the eternal, perfect, indivisible Identity that is your Identity and mine. But the genuine and *only* Identity is completely immune to any illusion. The genuine and *only* Identity is God identified, and God is not deluded.

Now we have arrived at the part played by the eye in this illusion. The eyes of man consist of an illusionary substance. They are not the genuine Substance of Spirit, Soul, Consciousness. Thus, they are not Substance at all. Being an illusion *about* genuine Vision, they can see and report only an illusory concept of that which they *appear* to see. This is why the false concept of vision reports separateness. This is the reason the eyes of man seem to see a distorted picture of that which is within the range of his limited vision.

Spirit, Consciousness, Life are one indivisible Whole, Entirety, All. Consciousness, being indivisible, cannot see division or separateness. All of us have heard of the eyes of Spirit. We have read about spiritual Vision. Well, the Eye of Spirit and spiritual Vision are one and the same Essence. The Eye of Spirit is Spirit. The Vision of Consciousness is Consciousness. There can be no separation *between* Consciousness and that which It sees because Consciousness is the very Essence which comprises that which It sees.

All that appears to be dense, solid, and dark is but the non-existent illusion reported by the eye of assumptive man. All that appears to be *confined* within certain forms is but an illusion about that which genuine Vision sees.

An illusion can see and report only the distortions of its own illusions. Genuine spiritual Vision can see and report only the genuine indivisible Essence of Its own Being. Spiritual Vision is Spirit seeing. Spirit seeing is enlightened Consciousness perceiving. Enlightened Consciousness perceiving is illumined Consciousness seeing — and being — that which It sees. This is visual illumination.

Please know that we have only touched upon some aspects of this phase of illumination. Right now, it is essential that we realize two tremendous facts.

First: That which the illusory eye of assumptive man sees consists of its own illusion.

Second: That which the Eye of Consciousness sees consists of Its own genuine Essence.

If these two points are clear, you are prepared to go on to the greater revelation of visual illumination in the following chapter.

Chapter IV

Visual Illumination

The Bible abounds in references to the Light. A comprehensive study of these references will be most enlightening. By contemplating the spiritual significance of these references, you will perceive that many who were called prophets or leaders were sometimes greatly illumined. Furthermore, you will realize that they experienced visual illumination.

An outstanding example of this fact may be read in Psalm 139:11,12:

> If I say, Surely the darkness shall cover me; Even the night shall be light about me. Yea, the darkness hideth not from thee; But the night shineth as the day: The darkness and the light are both alike to thee.

David was experiencing tremendous visual illumination when he sang this song of joy. Anyone who experiences great visual illumination will thoroughly comprehend just what David was perceiving.

There is a twofold meaning in this song of joy. First, David knew what it meant to be seemingly engulfed in darkness. He knew that sometimes this darkness would threaten to obliterate the Light he knew himself to be. But he had experienced visual illumination, and he *knew* that the darkness was but illusion. Whether the darkness appeared to be trouble or whether it appeared to be the darkness of the night was not important to David. What mattered to him was that he had seen Existence as It is, and he could not be deceived by *any* illusion of darkness. Second, he was aware that—even if he seemed to accept an illusion—the Light which he knew himself to be remained the same.

Many of us have had experiences which paralleled those of David. We too have felt as if the darkness would surely submerge us. But we too have experienced *being* the Light, and we are *not* deceived. We stand—no matter how grave the darkness may *appear* to be—in absolute conviction that the Light *does* exist. Furthermore, we *know* that even the illusion of darkness cannot obliterate the Light. We too have experienced the sudden radiance of visual illumination, right in the midst of what seemed to be stygian darkness. To us, the darkness and the Light *are* both alike because we *know* there is no darkness. All is Light.

Of course, there are many aspects of visual illumination. It is only in the greatest illumination that the Universe and all Existence is seen to be Light.

Let us now explore some other phases of visual illumination. No doubt you will recognize some of your own illumined experiences during this exploration. If so, never again will you misunderstand your *own* illumination. Neither will you limit your enlightened Consciousness by denying that already you *have* experienced illumination.

One aspect of visual illumination which frequently occurs has to do with color. It may be that suddenly the grass, the leaves, the flowers, and the shrubbery are perceived in much deeper, more intense hue. Paradoxically, this intensity of color also has a gentle, beautiful delicacy. You cannot describe it, but it is both intense and delicate. It never seems to be harsh or blatant. Always it glows, and there is a certain feeling of warmth about it. These intense colors are vibrant, and you have a sense of dynamic, living, loving Life, existing as color itself.

There is visual illumination in which the outlines of objects are exceedingly distinct. Objects stand out more clearly, and the delineation is more definite. It may or may not be an outline of very fine Light. Always, the beauty of that which you are seeing is greatly enhanced during visual illumination.

In some instances, the appearance of solidity will suddenly vanish, and you will see right through a supposedly solid object. This often happens with the body. After having attended a class in the Ultimate, one student reported the following experience. While shaving, he was standing in front of a mirror in line with a door. Suddenly he was aware that his body was transparent and that he was seeing the door right through the body. His illumination was so great that for many days his friends commented upon his radiant appearance. They apparently did not see the body as a transparency; but they *did* see the radiant glow that comprised his Body of Light. During this period, he went about his daily affairs quite normally and freely. Needless to say, he is an exceedingly enlightened student, and he understood the experience. He knew it was no hallucination.

There are illumined situations in which the indestructibility of all Substance is apparent. For instance, a lawn that has been mowed very close to the ground will be seen at its normal height. In this phase of illumination, grass that appears to be withered is suddenly seen to be gloriously green and *alive*. Broken boughs and dying leaves disappear, as perfect branches and fresh beautiful leaves are perceived.

Visual illumination *never* reveals imperfection. Rather it is that all *appearance* of imperfection is obliterated and what had appeared as imperfect is seen to be beautifully perfect. All that you see has a shiny, glowing appearance of newness and freshness.

Sometimes you will be aware of seeing everything in its completeness. The tree, branches, leaves, even the roots and the seed will be seen. A fruit tree will be complete, including the blossoms and the full ripe fruit. You will *never* see a withered branch or a barren tree in illumination. Neither will you see a disfigured form of any kind. The form is always beautiful and perfect, even as is the Substance of that which appears in form.

Right outside my study window stands a tall tree. I love this tree. The former owners of my house had used this tree for target practice, and it seemed to be dying. Furthermore, it appeared to have grown crookedly and was distorted in shape. Shortly after our arrival, I really *saw* the tree. I saw it as the beauty of Perfection. I saw it as beautifully symmetrical and with no horrible scars from the target practice. I saw it as eternal Life in form, completely new and fresh. I saw it as living Beauty, at the very height of its perfect being. Above all, I saw this tree in all its completeness. Although it was not supposed to be in bloom, I saw the blossoms. In addition to all of this, I saw the roots and the seed from which it had supposedly sprung.

It is noteworthy that the tree showed no solidity. On the contrary, it was a beautifully transparent Light in form. I will not attempt to describe it further, but I can tell you that now I *always* see this tree in all its pristine beauty. You will also be interested to know that even to those who apparently are unillumined, the tree appears more beautiful and symmetrical. And they see no sign of an injured tree. I could mention many such instances, but this will suffice to reveal two important facts: visual illumination reveals things as they are. The evidence of this illumination—even to the seemingly unillumined— is manifested as greater Perfection and beauty. In metaphysical terms, it would be said that the tree has been healed.

There is visual illumination in which you may suddenly find yourself in the presence of someone who has called for help. You may or may not have met this one. Often you will recognize just a silent plea for help from someone who imagines that he is appealing to a God other than his own God-Identity. If your Consciousness is sufficiently illumined, you will often be aware of that plea. After all, an illumined Consciousness is *not* personal. It is not the consciousness of a person. An illumined Consciousness is the infinite, impersonal Consciousness which is God. So a prayer to God is simply an opening of the Consciousness of the one who prays. Thus God, who is your enlightened Consciousness, is aware of this prayer.

When the one who calls for help is a student of the Ultimate, he is enlightened. In this event, he is very apt to see you when you are aware of being present with him. He may even *hear* you, if that is what seems necessary at the moment. One whom I love deeply was awakened by what appeared to be great pain. He cried out for help, and suddenly I was standing beside his bed, talking with him. He saw me, and he heard my voice. Instantly the pain was gone, and he fell asleep again. From a human standpoint, we were several hundred miles apart when this experience took place. Right here I must say that this loved one *had* to be illumined in order to see me and to hear my voice.

Although I mention just this one illumined experience, I assure you that there have been many others of a similar nature. I have no sense of projecting myself anywhere. I have no sense of going anywhere or of returning. It is just that suddenly I am there, and again suddenly I am here. When I am there, "there" is here to me. Yet "here" is here to me when I am conscious of being here.

Please do not mistake my purpose in telling these wonderful experiences. I would not infer that I am the only one who experiences this phase of illumination. On the contrary, there are many students of the Ultimate to whom this is a perfectly normal activity. Then, too, I have read and heard of enlightened ones who were seen and heard even though many miles seemed to intervene between this one and the one who seemed to need help. This is no new or novel experience. It has been going on throughout the centuries. The only reason it is not more generally known is that the participants are loath to mention it.

There has been great reticence about this because of a fear of being thought ridiculous or abnormal. The day is rapidly approaching when it will be realized that this is a perfectly normal experience. Illumination reveals what the physicists and scientists are only just discovering. Those engaged in the space effort are finding that *there are no spatial barriers.* Actually, there is no space. If "the things of the Spirit" had been nearly as important as "the foolish things of the world," these facts would have been known eons ago.

Let us now discuss that visual illumination which appears as color. There are many aspects in which color appears. Sometimes you will be aware of but one color. Again, you may see an infinite variety of colors. Even the body may appear to be a warm, glowing, golden shade, or it may appear to be a blue-white Light. Sometimes it will appear as a rose-like color, or it may be the color of pure white Light. When the body is seen to be transparent, it is generally seen as the Essence of pure Light, although it has no solidity. I can assure you of one thing: it is completely free of darkness. Furthermore, it is *always* beautiful, perfect, and symmetrical.

We know that the music we hear in aural illumination is completely unlike any earthly music. This same fact holds true in regard to the colors we see in visual illumination. We may see just one color, or we may see innumerable colors simultaneously. One of the most beautiful and satisfying colors is a glowing flame-like shade. Always, when this exquisite color appears, you will experience a tremendous surge of infinite Love. I might add that often this will take place when you have someone in Consciousness who has called for help. This flame-like sense of Love will invariably bring to light the perfection of that which had appeared to be imperfect. One thing I must make very clear:

> There is no spiritual "seeing" so fraught with power as is the Consciousness of being Love Itself.

When innumerable colors appear simultaneously, you will note that they are indivisible. There will be no line of demarcation between the colors. There will be no line where one color leaves off and another color begins. You will also notice that each color is specifically that particular color; yet each color includes *all* the infinite variety of colors which constitute the entire illumination. In other words, each color is complete as itself, yet its completeness includes all the colors in the Universe.

In this illumination, there is always a wonderful sense of being complete. You will realize that you *are* complete in all aspects of your being and body. You will also realize that you are complete because you are Completeness Itself. Many of you have had this experience, so you are aware of this glorious realization of being Completeness. It cannot be described in words. It can be understood only through having the experience. In any event, you who are yet to experience this illumination will understand it, and you will know that its spiritual significance is Completeness. Furthermore, you will know that it is your own Completeness, revealing Itself *to* Itself, *as* Itself.

There is another fact pertaining to illumination in color which is of vital importance. There is activity going on in, and as, these colors. It is intense activity. *It is nothing like vibration.* Rather it is as if the colors were a living, active Essence.

There is a reason for this appearance of intense activity. As you know, Life is active. Activity is Life. God being omnipresent, *Life* is omnipresent, for God is Life. Thus Life is God also. So when you are beholding the intense activity in and as these divine colors, you are beholding Life Itself. It is not surprising that you will be ecstatically alive as you experience this illumination.

There is another aspect of illumination as color that is a most glorious experience. This takes place when both visual and aural illumination are simultaneously experienced. You will see the most wonderful and indescribable colors while you are hearing the most sublime music. Now here is a seeming paradox: you actually seem to be *seeing* the music as well as hearing it. Conversely, you are aware of *hearing* the colors as well as seeing them. This is explained when you realize that there is no separation in Consciousness. It is the same Consciousness, whether It is manifested as seeing or hearing.

We hear much about the five physical senses. Actually, there are *no* physical senses. There is but one Sense, and that one is Consciousness. This one indivisible Sense may appear as seeing, hearing, touching, tasting, or smelling; but these are only certain aspects of Consciousness. We have often heard of a sixth sense, which is not so easily defined. Well, there are an untold number of activities of the one Consciousness. Each one is one specific, or distinct, activity of the one indivisible Consciousness.

There is the sense of direction, the sense of peace, of harmony, the sense of justice, and numerous other distinct but indivisible aspects of the one Consciousness. It is important to realize the inseparableness of Consciousness. There really is *no* line which separates hearing from seeing. Neither is there a line of demarcation between hearing, seeing, tasting, touching, or any other of the distinct aspects of Consciousness.

Time magazine printed a report that brings this fact into focus. This has to do with a psychiatrist who conducted an experiment in the presence of several of his colleagues. He blindfolded a young woman, and the blindfold was carefully checked. Then she opened a book, and by passing the fingertips of the right hand lightly across the page, she was able to read the text fluently. She proceeded to read a newspaper in the same way. Then they tested her with colored lights. She had stated that she could "feel" colors. They shone a red light on a light green book, making it look blue. She said it was blue. When the red light was turned off, she recognized the fact that the book was green.

That incident is very revealing. It points up a fact that is known to all who experience visual illumination. Vision is *not* confined to the small area of the eyes. There will come a day when it will be well known that Consciousness is unconfined, whether It is functioning as vision, hearing, or whatever.

When you are experiencing the greatest illumination, you are gloriously aware that the Consciousness you *are* is infinite. You *see* the Universe as It is. You see countless suns, moons, and planets. You have no sense of time or space. You are fully aware that you are inseparable from that which you see because the Consciousness which *sees* constitutes that which is seen.

In this full illumination, you may or may not be aware of the body; more often you are not. The light is so very bright; indeed, the light of the sun is pale in comparison with it. It is as if the brilliance of the Light conceals the outline of the body. Yet you are certainly aware that you exist and that you exist as an Identity. You do not lose your awareness of the fact that the body exists. It is just that it does not come to your attention at the moment. In like manner, you may know that a beautiful painting hangs upon the wall of your room. You may look at it a dozen times each day, and yet you do not really see it. Yet you know it is there, and if you suddenly feel that you would like to enjoy its beauty, you focus your attention upon the picture.

In full illumination, you are so absorbed in the infinite beauty and perfection of the Light that you do not notice the body at the moment. It is in this illumination that you are conscious of *being* all that you are seeing. It is useless to attempt to describe this experience. But those who do experience full illumination will know what I am trying to portray.

It could be said that full illumination is visual illumination. Yet it is more than just visual. It is as if all the various facets of Consciousness are *infinitely aware*, simultaneously. Complete illumination means a complete awareness of all Existence. It also means a complete awareness of *being* the Essence and the Activity of all that exists.

This experience may last for just a few seconds. Sometimes it is difficult to realize that it actually took place. Yet—if you are unafraid—it will be repeated again and again. Finally it may last for hours, or even days or weeks. One thing I know: you are aware that this is no hallucination. You know—beyond any doubt—that you have seen and experienced *being* Reality, and no one can shake your conviction that what you have seen and experienced is genuine.

If this were all, it might not be of supreme importance to experience full illumination. *But this is not all.* Your entire perspective is changed. Your daily experience becomes altogether different. You cannot live in the old way of materiality. Above all, you know the genuine meaning of Love, of Life, of Consciousness, and of Intelligence—and you find it necessary to act accordingly.

There is one point that must be emphasized here. The experience of full illumination does *not* mean that you live abnormally in any respect. You go about your daily affairs as usual; you do nothing ridiculous. You find that it is impossible to talk about what you are seeing and experiencing. Your friends and associates are not aware of anything different except in one way: you do not become disturbed, no matter *how* trying a situation may seem to be. You are joyous and free, and your work or profession goes smoothly. Some of the students say they realize that everything is being done *for* them, and they are completely free of any false sense of labor, struggle, or strain. There is no sense of weariness or exhaustion. Neither is there any sense of depletion. The activity of each day is effortless, although much more is accomplished than formerly seemed possible.

You *do* arrive at the point where your days and nights are a constant illumined experience. Oh, you are not in full illumination constantly. But you do see the wonderful glow of all Existence. You do see Perfection right where others imagine they see imperfection. You see Beauty where Its opposite is generally believed to be. You see Light where others seem to see darkness. And above all, you love—*oh, how you love.* You love everything you see. You love because you can do no other. You *are* Love. You know it. And you must be your Self. You can no more keep from loving than you can keep from breathing. Almost constantly you experience a warm, flame-like glow of infinite Love.

To those of you who have not yet consciously experienced being an illumined Identity, some questions may arise. These questions concern your attitude toward others. For instance, you may question something like this: Doesn't this experience set me apart from others? Doesn't it make me feel superior or higher than others? Doesn't it make me cold or impatient with the problems of others? The answer to each one of these questions is *No! No! No!* Quite the contrary is true.

You do *not* feel apart from others. You have perceived that there is one indivisible Consciousness, Life, Mind. You know that each one of us *is* this one Life, Consciousness, Mind. You have seen that this conscious, living Mind is inseparable and that the fact of being identified does not divide It into sections of Itself. It is not a matter of feeling one *with* others. It is far more than that. It is a matter of realizing that you *are* the same Consciousness, the same Life, the same Mind that is identified as everyone in existence.

Actually, to you the word *others* has a false connotation. You know there is no line of demarcation where they leave off and you begin. No, you are not one *with* anyone. The one you call "another" is exactly the same living, conscious, loving Mind that you are—and you *know it.*

There is biblical authority for this realization of Oneness. "At that day ye shall know that I am in my Father, and ye in me, and I in you" (John 14:20). Yes, "at that day" when illumination is consciously realized, you *do* realize that the Father and the Son are the same One. You are the Father, the Father is You, and there is *no* other. The One called "other" is the same Life, Consciousness, Mind that You are. This knowing precludes the possibility of being one *with* anyone. You can only recognize the same Mind, Consciousness, Life, Love that constitutes your Entirety.

Jesus was certainly fully illumined when he made the foregoing statement. He had gone all the way, and he knew there was no such thing as separateness. Certain it is that the one called Jesus had clearly shown his great love. He knew that he had to *be* Love in order to exist. He knew the meaning of impersonal Love, and he knew that Love is not something that can be given or withheld. Love simply *is*. Life, Consciousness, Mind, Love are all one and the same Consciousness.

Walking as an illumined being does *not* make you feel superior to those called "others." You never know the meaning of the word *humility* until you consciously experience illumination. How can you feel superior to or higher than your Self? You can't. You know that only because God *is*, can you be. You know there really is no one higher or lower than your Self. You are aware that the one whom you call "another" is the very same God-Consciousness — and *equally* this same Consciousness — that you are. You limit *no* one. The whole basis of the Ultimate is that each and every Identity is equally the one and *only* Identity, which is God.

No indeed, you do *not* feel cold or impatient with the problems of those called "others." Remember, you are Love. You *know* how genuine and formidable these apparent problems can seem to be. True, you know that there is no problem and no one actually experiencing a problem. But you do *not* ignore the fact that the appearance of a problem seems most real to the one who has accepted it as genuine.

It is as if you were standing beside someone who was dreaming. *You* know that the dream is completely spurious. You know that this one is completely immune to the dream. You also know the nature of the dream. If it is a pleasant dream, you will probably feel it is better to let it continue; but if it is a tragic nightmare, you certainly will attempt to awaken him.

Oh, you will do this most gently. Whatever you do, it is done in gentleness and in Love. Love is *always* gentle. Love is compassionate. But Love does not descend to the level of the nightmare. Love stays awake because only a Consciousness which is clear and alert can see clearly enough to dispel the nightmare. Love and Intelligence are inseparably One. Therefore, the Love that *is* Mind acts intelligently. To accept the nightmare that seems to be the experience of a supposititious dreamer would be to manifest Love without Intelligence.

Sympathy is *not* Love. Sympathy is a so-called human emotion. Sympathy never eliminates a nightmare. Compassion is Love. Compassion is a deep spiritual understanding of the seeming needs of the one called "other." Compassion speaks and acts lovingly and gently, but it also acts intelligently. Compassion is a realization of what the problem seems to be, an understanding of how real and tragic it appears, and a joyous consent to cancel the mistaken sense. It is sufficient just to see and to be the Consciousness which knows that Perfection is All.

The glorious ways in which visual illumination may be experienced are innumerable. I have mentioned only a few of these aspects. Many books would be required to present thoroughly the infinite variety in which visual illumination is experienced.

There is one most important aspect of this illumination which has been barely introduced in this chapter. This is illumination in which the body is clearly seen. The visible "Body of Light" is of great importance. Because this subject is of such vital spiritual significance, the entire next chapter will be devoted to the eternal, immutable, glorious Body of Light.

Chapter V

The Body of Light

Enlightened Consciousness is spiritual Consciousness. Spiritual Consciousness sees the things of Spirit. The illusion called a mortal consciousness sees its own illusion. Being an illusion itself, it can see only the substances, forms, and activities of its own delusions.

We know that a delusion must be a delusion about *something*. There can be no illusion about *nothing*. So the illusory picture of darkness, density, matter, is an illusion *about* Spirit, Light, Consciousness, Intelligence, Life.

There is no darkness or solidity existing as Spirit, Light, Consciousness, Intelligence, Life. Yet these aspects of Existence comprise *Substance*. The illusory substance that appears to be solid, dark matter is but an illusion *about* the genuine Substance which is comprised of Spirit, Light, Life, Mind, Consciousness.

Often we hear or read the word *darkness* used to define ignorance. Ignorance would be an absence of knowledge pertaining to something which does exist. An illusory concept called the mind of man is *not* Mind. It is *not* Intelligence. Thus, it must be an assumed absence of knowledge of that which *does* exist. This darkness must, of necessity, see darkness.

Being dense—ignorant of genuine Existence—it must see only the objects and delineations of its own density or ignorance.

The body which appears to be material is constituted of an illusory substance. It is an illusion forming its own objects and delineations out of its own ignorance. Solidity, darkness, density are comprised of an illusory sense of substance. This illusory ignorance of that which *does* constitute Substance *is all there is of that which appears to be material.*

It is vitally important to realize one fact pertaining to the illusion versus that which does exist: Mind has no awareness of an illusion. Consciousness is Its own immunity to any illusory concepts *about* It. Consciousness, being All, is only aware of Itself. Conversely, the illusory mind of man is only aware of *itself.* "For what man knoweth the things of a man, save the spirit of man which is in him? even so the things of God knoweth no man, but the Spirit of God" (I Cor. 2:11). There can be *no* intermingling of the genuine and the spurious. The genuine *is.* The spurious *is not.* The Consciousness that does exist has no awareness of that which does not exist. In other words, God is conscious *only* of Itself.

The sun is completely untouched by the dark clouds that seem so dense and formidable. It is its own immunity to darkness. It just goes right on shining as its own light. Thus it is with enlightened Consciousness, which is the *only* Consciousness. It is completely immune to any illusory appearances of darkness. It just goes right on *being* the illumined Consciousness which It is.

There is a Body of Light. This Body is comprised entirely of Consciousness, Life, Mind, Love. We have heard and read much about the spiritual Body. The Body of Spirit does exist, and It is the *only* Body. The Body of Spirit is Consciousness, Life, Mind, Love in form. As stated before, Consciousness is Spirit, and Consciousness, Life, Love, Intelligence are inseparably One. This One is God.

The genuine and *only* Consciousness in existence sees the Body of Light. Enlightened Consciousness is the only Consciousness that exists. The only Body in existence is comprised of the *only* Consciousness in existence, and this is *enlightened* Consciousness.

There is nothing supernatural about this Body of Light, and neither is there anything mysterious about It. Seen as It is, It is a perfectly normal body. But It can be seen only by the Consciousness which is Light Itself. The one called Jesus certainly saw the Body of Light, and he was not alone in this perception. There is nothing new about the visibility of the Body of Light. It has been seen again and again by enlightened ones, and this fact is recorded in many ancient religious writings.

Jesus said, "The light of the body is the eye: if therefore thine eye be single, thy whole body shall be full of light" (Matt. 6:22). The eye is comprised of Consciousness. If you are perceiving as illumined Consciousness, you will actually see and experience the Body of Light. However, Jesus added, "But if thine eye be evil, thy whole body shall be full of darkness. If therefore the light that is in thee be darkness, how great is that darkness!" (Matt. 6:23).

Yes, the Light already exists *in* you because the Light exists *as* you. But if the "you" that *seems* to see is in darkness — in ignorance of that which stands before you — then you are completely ignorant. This would mean that you were not Mind, but absence of Mind. This is impossible because there is no absence of Mind. Mind is God and God is Omnipresence. In Omnipresence there are no vacuums. So even the appearance of darkness is illusion. If you do not consciously see the Body of Light, you are not really seeing the body at all.

Now we have arrived at what seems to be a paradox. It is possible that you may not appear consciously to see the Body of Light. Yet you actually *do* see the Body of Light. You cannot help seeing It if you are conscious, and you *are* conscious. Nothing can be conscious *but* Consciousness. Just as surely as you are aware that you exist, you are Consciousness being conscious. So actually, the illusion that you do *not* see the Body of Light has no basis in fact. Again, it is an illusion deluding itself. An illusion is nothing, and there is *no* deluded one. So an illusion is *nothing seeing nothing.*

Oh beloved one, do you see what we are doing here? We are dissolving the mist — mistaken concept — which has seemed to bind you and blind you to the glorious heaven which is right here and now. The illusory mist is being dispersed in order that you may see and *consciously be* the enlightened One, which you already *are.*

That which you have been reading here is no mere theory or work of fiction. It is absolute fact. It is true. If you can accept its truth, you may be sure that you *can* see things as they are, including the Body of Light.

Let us now enter into a more thorough discussion of the Body of Light. We have perceived that the Light is illumined Consciousness. We have also seen that Consciousness comprises the body. You know that you are conscious and that only Consciousness is conscious. Therefore, it naturally follows that the Substance of the body is the very Consciousness which is conscious *as your awareness of existing.*

Yes, the body consists of the Consciousness you are. But you will remember the inseparability of Consciousness, Life, Mind, Love. Thus, you will perceive that the body must be constituted of the Consciousness you are, the Life you are, the Intelligence you are, and the Love you are. If the conscious, living, loving Mind you are is enlightened — and It is — then the body is a Body of Light, comprised of your own enlightened Consciousness.

Right at this point, some positive, unequivocal facts must be stated. There are *not* two of you — one that is enlightened Consciousness and another that is unenlightened consciousness. There is just the one *you,* and this one is Spirit, or illumined Consciousness. Furthermore, you do not have two bodies—one a Body of Spirit and another an illusory body of solidity. We are not trying to enlighten an unenlightened consciousness. There is no such consciousness. We are not trying to change a body of darkness into a Body of Light. There is no body of darkness. Actually, we are not trying to do *anything.* We know that nothing could be done about something that does not exist. So the whole purpose of this book is to be fulfilled as your "eyes are opened" and you perceive your genuine and *only* Life, Substance, Being, and Body.

Just about now, you may be asking some questions, and they may be quite pertinent questions, too. For instance: Why is it important that I see and experience the Body of Light? I just want to be more healthy, wealthy, or more joyous and at peace. How is this perception of the Body of Light going to help me in my daily life and experience? How can this theory—beautiful as it is—be practical in my life?

If perception of the Body of Light were merely an experience isolated from your daily living, there would be no purpose in writing this book. If this were only a beautiful theory, you might just as well read one of the lovely Greek myths or a fairy story. However, if the perception of the Body of Light and the Universe of Light is a realization of that which is true, it is provable. Anything that is true can be proved. That which is not true cannot be proved.

In order that anything be proven, it must be evident, and this evidence must be *apparent* in daily life and experience. When—through the perception of the Body of Light—a healthy body is apparent, we actually are seeing and experiencing the proof that the Body of Light is a true, genuine body. This is proof that what we are perceiving is true.

When a healthy body is experienced—right where an unhealthy body had appeared to be—you may rest assured that this Truth is apparent in daily life and experience. This is exactly what has been taking place through the enlightened, conscious perception of the Body of Light. So this spiritual perception is more than a beautiful theory. It is practical.

You may discover just how practical is this Truth through the study and contemplation of the words and works of Jesus. For instance, to the man who apparently had a withered hand, he said, "Stretch forth thine hand. And he stretched it forth; and it was restored whole, like as the other" (Matt. 12:13). Jesus did *not* change a withered hand into a normal hand. *No one can change something which is not true into something which is true.* Jesus saw the hand that was not withered. He didn't give a treatment to a withered hand. Rather he saw only that which was already whole and perfect, needing nothing to become the perfection which it already was.

In short, Jesus saw the Body of Light rather than a body of darkness, solidity, density. Jesus' perception of the Body of Light revealed the perfection that already existed. Furthermore, this perfection was *apparent* to the man with a withered hand and those gathered around Jesus. This is quite practical, isn't it? No mere theory would have brought into view a perfect hand instantly, right where a withered hand had appeared to be present.

This incident is but one of many in which Jesus made a simple statement of what was true, and omnipresent Perfection was revealed, perceived, and evident. To the man who was called a leper, he simply said, "Be thou clean. And immediately his leprosy was cleansed" (Matt. 8:3). Did Jesus really *see* a leprous body? Indeed he did not. He saw the pure, uncontaminated Body of Light. The evidence of that which Jesus saw was instantly apparent. This evidence did not come *into* existence. *It was already the established fact.*

You will remember that the ruler of the synagogue believed his daughter to be dead. Yet Jesus simply took her by the hand and said, "Maid, arise. And her spirit came again, and she arose straightway" (Luke 8:54-55). Jesus *knew* the genuine nature of the body. He did not accept a *kind* of body that was destructible or perishable. He perceived the eternal, immutable Body of Light. Jesus made one significant statement before entering the so-called death chamber. He said, "Weep not; she is not dead, but sleepeth" (Luke 8:52). From this statement, it is apparent that Jesus did not accept the illusion of a body that had died. He knew that the Body of Light could not die because it was never born. As evidence that this is true, we have the record that the maid was discovered to be alive.

The scene enacted before the tomb of Lazarus is profoundly significant. Lazarus was said to be dead and in the tomb four days. Yet Jesus simply said, "Lazarus, come forth" (John 11:43). Lazarus did come forth, and he was not minus a body. The body of Lazarus was *apparent* to those standing around that tomb. It was evident as a perfectly normal, healthy, alive body. Yes, Jesus' perception of the eternal Body of Light proved to be *very* practical.

It has been said that these seemingly miraculous healings were all ended when Jesus no longer walked the earth. It has also been said that Jesus was the only one who could perform these wonderful works. But Jesus himself said, "He that believeth on me, the works that I do shall he do also; and greater works than these shall he do" (John 14:12). From this statement, it is apparent that Jesus did not expect the so-called miracles to cease when he was no longer visible.

We know that Paul and Peter continued to perform the works of Jesus. This is a matter of record in our Bible. Witness the account of the lame beggar at the gate of the temple called Beautiful. Peter did not hesitate to take this man by the hand and tell him to "rise up and walk" (Acts 3:6). Peter might as well have said. "What is stopping you? You *are* perfect, and your body is perfectly capable of walking." In any event, the supposedly lame man leapt, walked, and went with them into the temple. Paul had much this same kind of experience at Lystra. To the man who was said to have been born lame, Paul merely said, "Stand upright on thy feet. And he leaped and walked" (Acts 14:10).

Of course, it may be said that these episodes took place years ago and that there are no evidences of such miracles in our modern-day experiences. Nothing could be farther from the truth. There *are* such experiences going on every day. Jesus' promise of greater works is being fulfilled. Oh, you don't read about it in the newspapers, and it is rarely mentioned in the current magazines. But it does take place. Furthermore, these assumed miracles have been taking place for many years. Why these glorious events are not publicized is not important. What is important is the fact that the ability to perceive and to reveal the perfect Body is present today, just as it was present when Jesus performed his wonderful works.

It seems paradoxical that this power to reveal the perfect Body should have been present all through the years, yet it is so little known today. One cannot help but question why this should be true. There *is* an answer to this question, and that answer lies in our failure to be illumined sufficiently to perceive the Body of Light. Furthermore, even when the Body of Light has been seen, there has been an unwillingness to accept It as genuine. In fact, sometimes there has been an unwillingness to admit the reality of the experience itself. It has been believed to be a hallucination or something abnormal.

The Body of Light is no hallucination. It is genuine. It is eternal, changeless, and forever perfect. It is never born; It does not mature, deteriorate, or age, and It can never die. Our only hope of experiencing uninterrupted perfect health, strength, and perfection lies in our enlightened perception of this eternally perfect Body.

It is a documented fact that there have been many healings that have seemed miraculous. Whenever a so-called healing has taken place, *the body remained but the disease, or abnormality, vanished.* Obviously, the mistake lies not in or on the body; it is in the failure to perceive the body as it is. This failure is due to the fact that we tend to judge the condition of the body by the way it appears to the human mind and the human vision. The assumptive human mind can *never* know the Body of Light. The human vision can never see the Body of Light. It takes *enlightened* Consciousness to know, or to see, the Body of Light.

If we are to be entirely free of all trouble and inharmony of any kind, illumination, or enlightened Consciousness, is requisite. Thus, it behooves us to recognize and accept enlightened Consciousness. Above all, it is necessary for us to accept the fact that enlightened Consciousness is our Consciousness, *right here and now.*

You will remember Jesus' promise that "greater works" were to be performed. It would seem impossible that there could be any works performed greater than those performed by Jesus. But he knew what these greater works were to be, and he knew they would be performed. These greater works are the illumination which reveals uninterrupted perfection to be a *constant* fact, and the evidence of this fact is the eternal, perfect Body of each and every Identity in existence.

Of course, the next question would be: How can I experience illumination? What can I do that will enable me to be an enlightened being? The answers to these questions are:

> Stop denying the fact that you are already an enlightened Consciousness. Admit that you must be somewhat enlightened in order to be conscious at all.

I have never known anyone to experience full illumination by a denial that he was an illumined being. This would be a denial of the Christ Itself, for the Christ-Consciousness is an illumined Consciousness.

The first step in the realization of conscious illumination is the acceptance of the Christ. This is true because it is the Christ-Consciousness which is completely illumined Consciousness. The illumined

Christ-Consciousness is your Consciousness and mine. The illumined Christ-Consciousness is the Consciousness of everyone who is conscious. No matter how unaware of this fact one may seem to be, the fact remains that the illumined Christ-Consciousness is the *only* genuine Consciousness in existence. Can you accept this fact?

Can you perceive that it is possible for *you* to see as Jesus saw and to act as Jesus acted? If so, you have taken the first step in conscious, full illumination.

Paradoxically, the first step toward full illumination is the *only* step that can be taken. No mental gymnastics will bring illumination into your experience.

No concentrated meditation will reveal the eternal Body of Light. No mental imaging will reveal this Body, and no attempt to visualize It will produce It. It is a mistake to attempt any of these mental exercises. They will not work, and they lead to much confusion—or something worse than that. Certain it is that any mental effort along this line will tend to delay the revelation of the eternal, perfect Body of Light.

Having taken the first and *only* step toward conscious, complete enlightenment, we have accepted the unequivocal fact: we *are* illumined Christ-Consciousness. It may *seem* that we are not aware of being enlightened or that at least we are aware of very little enlightenment. Yet we *have* accepted the fact that we are the Consciousness that is enlightened. This is the "little leaven that leaveneth the whole lump" (Gal. 5:9).

It is noteworthy that Jesus spoke of the kingdom as being like leaven which was hidden in three measures of meal "till the whole was leavened" (Matt. 13:33). This is an apt description of what takes place when one recognizes and admits the illumined Christ-Consciousness to be one's only Consciousness. The figure 3 has always symbolized completeness. The term "three measures of meal" signifies the fact that complete illumination inevitably follows the "little leaven," or the first acceptance of the fact that one's Consciousness is illumined.

Throughout the years we have been told to accept the Christ. Even orthodoxy exhorts its followers to let the Christ be in the heart of man. Now we *know* the spiritual significance behind this admonition. To accept the Christ is to accept illumined Consciousness as our own Consciousness. No matter how small may seem to be our awareness of this *fact*, the very acceptance of it must ultimately reveal that the Consciousness we are is fully illumined.

To recognize that the Christ-Consciousness is *your* Consciousness means to accept the fact that you can see as Jesus saw; you can know as he knew; you can experience as he experienced; and you can *be* what he was, and is. The acceptance of the Christ-

Consciousness is not an activity of the assumptive human mind. Only the Mind which is God can recognize and accept the Christ-Consciousness. The Mind which is God is the Christ-Consciousness. *This* is why Jesus saw only perfection where others seemed to see imperfection. The Consciousness which is God — the Christ-Consciousness — has no awareness of imperfection. It has no awareness of *anything* other than Itself, because God is All.

There can be no doubt that the disciples were aware of the necessity to realize that the Christ-Mind was the Mind of each Identity in existence. Paul flatly stated, "But we have the mind of Christ" (I Cor. 2:16). He made another statement which is equally important: "Let this mind be in you, which was also in Christ Jesus" (Phil. 2:5).

Yes, the Christ-Mind, the illumined Christ-Consciousness, is your own Consciousness. You do not have to make It become your Mind. You do not even have to make It become any more complete as your Consciousness. The Christ-Mind is complete as your Mind right now. In order to be aware of this fact, it is necessary only to accept it to be true. It already is — "let it be."

The subject for this chapter is the Body of Light. It may seem odd to you that we have dwelt so much upon the illumined Consciousness, or Christ-Consciousness. It has been necessary to comprehend the Christ-Consciousness and to perceive that this illumined Consciousness is *your* Consciousness, right here and now. This was essential to the perception and comprehension of the Body of Light. You see, it is the illumined Christ-Consciousness that sees and experiences this Body of Light.

Now let us return to the Body of Light. We will explore this subject until it is completely clarified. Often the question arises whether or not the Body of Light has form. Indeed it does. But the outline, or delineation, of the form does not confine the Light which is this Body. Any attempt to describe this Body would necessarily be faulty. It must be seen and experienced in order to be fully understood. Furthermore, the *only* Vision that can see It is illumined Vision, and the *only* one who can see It is an illumined Christ-Consciousness. However, it is possible to present a simile that may aid you in perceiving more clearly what constitutes this radiant, eternal, perfect Body of Light.

Can you imagine a room that is ablaze with a glorious light? Distributed in this room are many transparent crystal globes. The light in the room shines right *through* the clear crystal of each globe. There is nothing about the outline of the globe that keeps the light out of the globe. Furthermore, there is nothing that can confine the light within each globe. The so-called outside and the inside, the above and the below, are all the same light.

Of course, you know that the globe exists and that it has outline, or delineation. But unless something causes you to focus your attention specifically upon the globe, you will not even notice it. The outline of the globe is not of primary importance. What is important is the light itself.

These globes may appear in many distinct shapes and sizes. Each globe is *that* specific globe and no other. Yet the light within any specific globe does not differ *in the least* from the light within another globe. No one of the globes can divide or separate the light in the entire room. The light is equally intense at every point throughout this imaginary room. The light is no more intense within one globe than it is within another. The light within the globe is no more or less intense than is the entire light throughout the room.

We can use this as a simile of the Body of Light as It exists in the Universe of Light. This Universe is a Universe of Light. It is a beautifully radiant Universe. Anyone who experiences full illumination will vouch for this fact. It is only an illusion that makes it *appear* to be both light and dark. The Light which constitutes this Universe is present in equal intensity everywhere. There is no greater or lesser Light anywhere. There is not even so much as a pinpoint in which this Light does not shine in equal intensity. And there are no vacuums, or areas of darkness, in this universal Light.

The Light that constitutes the Universe is eternal. The eternality of this Light is never interrupted, not even for one split second. It never began and It can never end. It is never any more or any less bright. It is immutable, infinite, and eternal.

One more point should be perceived here: this Light is *active*. It is in constant, intense activity. More will be said about the activity of the universal Light later in this book. Just now, our purpose is to call your attention to the fact that the Universe is constituted of radiant Light.

There is another aspect of the Universe of Light which we must now discuss. Within this infinite Light is infinite variety. Please note here that the word *within* is used only to denote that which exists as this universal Light. There is nothing outside the Universe because It is Infinity Itself. Nevertheless, this Universe is constituted of an infinite variety of Its own Essence. This variety does not mean that there is any more or any less Light existing as *any* specific aspect of the Light. It is just that the universal Light is identified as an infinite variety of the infinite Light which It is.

Each star is a distinct aspect of the universal Light. Each planet, each bird, and each grain of sand is included in this infinite variety. In fact, everything that exists as form, or Essence in form, exists as an aspect of the infinite variety which constitutes this Universe. One aspect in which this universal Light appears is the Body of Light.

Now let us return to the simile of the room and the crystal globes. Compare the radiant Light within the room to the Universe of Light. Then compare the outline of each globe to the form of the body. The universal Light is not excluded from the body. The delineation of the form does not shut the Light *out* of the body. Neither does it dim this Light or divide It in any way. The Light delineated by the form is identically the same Light that constitutes the universal Light. In other words, the Essence, outlined by the form, is identically the same Essence that constitutes the Universe.

The universal Light is unconfined. It is not contained *within* the form. It is only when your attention is focused upon the form that you are specifically aware of the form of the body. In fact, in great illumination you may not be aware of the body at all. It is as if the Light were so intense that it concealed the form of the body. In any event, you may rest assured that in great illumination, your attention is not focused upon the body. You are so *aware* of the glorious, infinite Light that *It* is the important realization at the moment. Furthermore, you are aware of *being* this radiant Light you are seeing.

Now, you may have some further questions about this Body of Light. For instance: Is It active? Yes. Does It have weight? No. Does It function as the illusory body of matter functions? It functions, but the functions are *not* what they appear to be in the body made of illusion. Perhaps your greatest questions will be: How do I know that I have a body? And why do I have a body?

You know that you have a body because you are conscious. You are aware of the body, and awareness is Consciousness. You have a body because the body is necessary to your completeness. This is a complete Universe. The complete Universe is God. The Completeness which is God *has* to be identified as what God is—namely, Completeness. If the body were not necessary to your completeness, you would never have had an awareness of body. That which is necessary to your completeness right now is *eternally* necessary to your completeness. There is never one second in which God is incomplete. Thus, there is never a second in which *you* are incomplete. If you could be bodiless, you would be incomplete. If *you* were incomplete, God would be incomplete, *for your completeness is necessary in order that God be complete.*

This is the reason why you may rest assured that you are never without a body. Furthermore, you will *never* be without a body. The Body of Light is an eternal Body. It never began, and above all, *It never began to be your Body.* It can never end, and *It can never cease to be your Body.* You see, It is essential to your completeness. If it is essential to your completeness this moment, It is eternally essential to your completeness. If there could be a period in which you were without a body, in that period you would be incomplete. If there could be a moment in which you were incomplete, in that moment God would be incomplete. This, of course, is an impossibility.

It is apparent that we are not alluding to a "born" body when we speak of your eternal Body. Do not be deceived. You do not have two bodies—one a Body of Light and the other a body of darkness. You have but one Body, and this is the eternal, birthless Body of Light. It was this eternal, perfect Body of Light which Jesus perceived, and it is this eternal perfect Body of Light which *you* perceive when you are illumined. It is this eternal Body which existed as *your* Body before the illusion called birth seemed to overtake you.

It is the eternal Body of Light that was seen by the disciples on the Mount of Transfiguration. There stood Moses and Elijah, and their Bodies of Light were visible to the three disciples. No doubt there had been many friends and relatives who imagined they had buried the bodies of Moses and Elijah years before the event of the transfiguration. But had they? Indeed no.

The Body of Light is the *only* Body, and It can never be buried in the earth. For that matter, what is the substance of the earth in which these assumptive bodies of solidity are supposed to be buried? The Substance of the earth is identically the same Essence as is the Body of Light. How, then, could the Body of Light be buried? It can't. It isn't buried, and It never has been buried. Furthermore, It never will be buried. No one exists who can bury Light. And there is nothing existing that can hide or conceal Light. No, you do *not* have two bodies.

Now we have arrived at an important revelation pertaining to the Body of Light. We must know what constitutes the Light which comprises this Body. The quickest and most simple way to explain the Essence we call Light is simply to say It is God. This would be telling the truth, because It really *is* God. It has to be God, for God is All. God being All—Everything—there can be nothing existing that is not God. But if we do not know what God is, this explanation does not help us very much. Specifically, let us discover what God is as the Body of Light.

There are innumerable synonyms for God. In fact, God being All, *every noun in our vocabulary should be a synonym for God.* Among innumerable synonyms, we frequently hear the words *Life, Mind, Spirit,* and *Love.* It is true that God is Life. It is also true that God is Mind. But Mind is Intelligence, so we understand that God is Intelligence. God is Spirit, and Spirit is Consciousness. It follows that God is Consciousness. God is Love, and the Love which is God is evidenced in ways that are all unsuspected in the illusory picture of existence.

God being Life and God being All, the *only* Life in existence has to be God. Now God, Life, has to live *as* Something, and this Something has to be alive. It is. This Something that is alive is the Body of Light.

Life is as indivisible as is Light. So Life does not divide Itself into confined areas of Itself. The Life that lives as the body is not confined *to* the body. Rather it is the universal Light—the universal Life—which is alive as the Life of the Body of Light. Life and Light are identical. So the Body of Light is the Body of Life. It is true that God is eternal Life. This being true, the Body of Light—or Life—has to be an eternal Body. The Body of Light is an eternal Body, and It is alive eternally, without beginning or ending.

It is clear now that Life is the Essence of your Body of Light. But there can be no unconscious Life. All Life is *conscious* Life because Life and Consciousness are inseparable. There is no line of demarcation where Life leaves off and Consciousness begins. The Body of Light is not only a Body that is alive; it is also a Body that is conscious. We have arrived at the fact that the Body of Light is comprised of Life that is conscious and Consciousness that is alive.

As stated before, we have heard much about the spiritual body. The word *Spirit* has had a very vague connotation for many of us. Actually, Spirit and Consciousness are the same Essence. So the spiritual body is the conscious, living Body of Light. Consciousness is God, and God is eternal. Thus, Consciousness is an eternal Existent. The Consciousness which is the Essence of the Body of Light is eternal; thus, It is eternally conscious. We can now perceive that eternal, living Consciousness comprises the Essence of the Body of Light.

Mind is God. Mind is a universal Existent. Intelligence is inseparable from living Consciousness. This is true because God is indivisible. There can be no Body of Light without Intelligence or Mind. Thus, the Body of Light consists of living, conscious Intelligence; or conscious, living Intelligence; or intelligent, conscious Life. It makes no difference how it is said or written, the fact remains that indivisible, conscious, living Intelligence constitutes the Body of Light.

We have said that God is Love. Intelligent, living Consciousness is inseparable from Love because God is not divisible. There are no outlines dividing and separating Life from Consciousness, Mind from living Consciousness, or conscious living Mind from Love. So Love is also the Essence of the Body of Light. When we know — really know — what Love is, we will realize the importance of the fact that Love is essential as the Essence of the Body of Light. We are going to investigate the word *Love* during the course of this book, and it will become very clear that Love is essential to the completeness of the Body of Light.

We have said that universal Light is present in equal intensity everywhere and eternally. This is but one way of saying that the Light is complete — as all that It is — everywhere and eternally. God is the universal Light, and God is Perfection. Furthermore,

God is complete Perfection. God is also all Beauty. So Beauty and Perfection are inseparable. Life, Intelligence, Consciousness, Beauty, Perfection are inseparably One, and this inseparable One constitutes the Body of Light.

Another synonym for God is Reality, or Truth. This means that God is all that is real; God is all that is true. All that is true is Truth, and Truth alone is real. So the Body of Light must, of necessity, consist of Reality, or Truth. Every Truth is an *eternal* Truth. Everything that is real is an *eternal* Existent. The conscious, living Intelligence which constitutes the Body of Light must also be the very Essence of that which is eternally real, that which is eternally true. When Jesus said, "I am the truth," he was not excluding his body from the Truth he knew himself to be. The true, or genuine, body is the *only* body. The real and *only* body is the eternal, perfect Body of Light. There is no other body.

The outline of this perfect Body of Light does not consist of a substance other than the Light Itself. Rather it is the Light delineating Its own Essence. There is nothing solid, dense, or dark about this delineation. It is all Light, and when It is seen *as It is*, you will clearly perceive how it is—and why it is— that the delineation and the Essence of the Body of Light are identical. Those of you who have seen this Body of Light, or who do see It, will understand why it is impossible to explain further the paradox of an outline which is not really an outline at all.

Do not be discouraged if you have not experienced seeing the Body of Light. *You will see It.* In fact, you may be fully illumined before you have finished reading this book. In any event, you may be assured that complete illumination is *inevitable.* You would not have come this far in your search unless you were going to go all the way. *Just refrain from trying to visualize anything.*

Refuse to *try* to become completely illumined. Accept the "little leaven" which leavens the entire Consciousness. Accept the fact that you *are* the illumined Christ-Consciousness right here and now.

Even though it may not appear at the moment that you are the Christ-Light, you *can* recognize the fact that "the Mind that was in Christ Jesus" is in you. Indeed It is. Because, you see, *It is your only Mind.*

Chapter VI

The Universe of Light

To some individuals, the Universe seems to be bounded by their own immediate environment. Others consider the Universe to be our Earth planet. Those of wider perception envision the Universe as the stars, planets, etc., which are included in our galaxy. Then there are those with vision great enough to perceive that our galaxy does not include all that constitutes the Universe. These are the ones who are beginning to dissolve the seeming bonds of limitation, and they are well along on their way to a comprehension of the irrefutable fact: the Universe is boundless, immeasurable, and indefinable by *any* circumference.

The limitless, boundless Universe is God. This is an unequivocal fact. Furthermore, it is a fact that must be accepted if we are going to experience completely enlightened Consciousness. We have made the statement "God is All." This is an absolute statement of fact. God *is* All. But if God is All, then All is God. This being true, it follows that God *must* be the Universe. If God is All, this infinite Universe must consist of just what God is, or else there is no Universe.

No assumptive human mind could grasp the Infinity which comprises the Universe. Neither can an assumed human mind perceive the Infinitude which is God. The assumptive intelligence that is called a human mind is bound within its own limitations. Its very nature is limited because its life span is limited. It is supposed to be born, to be centered in a brain, and, after a limited number of years, it is supposed to die. Being illusory by its very nature, it must of necessity be limited. *Any* illusion must have a beginning; thus, it must also have an ending.

There is nothing limited about the Universe. Neither is there anything limited about the Mind that perceives the boundless, immeasurable nature of the Universe. If It were not God, it is inconceivable that the Universe could be boundless in terms of time and space.

If we are going to continue saying, "God is All," we are going to have to accept the fact that God is the Universe. This means that God is the entire Essence and activity of each star, planet, sun, moon, and of each galaxy which constitutes the Universe. But this is not all: God must be the Substance and the activity of our Earth planet. It is well to remember that this Earth planet is just another planet to those who may inhabit the planet Mars. No doubt they are just as curious about us as we are about them. In any event, our point is: if God be All, God constitutes the Essence and the activity of everything in existence throughout Infinity and Eternity.

In Webster's unabridged dictionary, you will find the term *homogeneous atmosphere*. The definition for this term is given as: "Atmosphere having the same specified density throughout, and a given surface pressure." If you can translate this expression into spiritual terms, you will realize more clearly *the Nature of God* existing as the Universe.

All that God is, is eternally present in equal intensity throughout Infinity. It *has* to be thus, because God is Infinity. Thus, the Universe is Infinity. God is complete. This means that the Universe is complete. In order to be complete, the Universe must, of necessity, consist of everything that is necessary to *comprise* this completeness.

We know that there are stars, planets, galaxies, suns, and moons in existence. We know also that there is an infinite variety of stars, planets, galaxies, etc. It is generally recognized that no two of the planets, no two of the stars, are exactly the same — either in size, in shape, or in atmospheric and other aspects. What is *not* generally known is that astronomers often speak of the body of the planet Mars or the body of another planet. In fact, the astronomers consider each star and planet to be that distinct body and no other.

It is obvious that the Universe consists of an infinite variety of aspects of Itself. There are innumerable heavenly bodies of various distinct natures and characteristics. Each star, each planet is distinctly that star or that specific planet. Yet each star is the Universe; each sun, each moon, each planet is distinguishable of itself. Consequently, each one is the Universe. It has to be this way because the Universe is the very Essence of everything which constitutes Its entirety.

The body of each star and each planet certainly *appears* to be a body of density. The body of our Earth planet seems to be a mass of ever-changing solidity. But is it? Let us discover whether or not these bodies that appear to be so solid really are the way they appear to be. We have realized that God, the Universe, is present in equal intensity through Its entirety. We know that this Universe is complete. The fact of being complete necessitates the inclusion of all that is necessary to completeness.

Each star, each planet, sun, moon, galaxy, etc., is essential to the completeness which constitutes the Universe. There are no bodiless stars or planets. There are no formless suns or moons. So there *are* bodies included in the Completeness which is God, the Universe. God is not dense; God is not solid; God is not dark; and God does not change. So the bodies which appear to be changing, solid, dark, dense bodies are not the way they appear to be. These bodies can be no more solid or dense than is God—because God *is* the very Essence that comprises each one of them. God does not solidify Itself through the incident of being the body of a planet. God does not become density or darkness by reason of being the body of the Earth planet. God is a homogeneous God. God remains the same Essence, despite the fact that this Essence is evidenced as the body of a star, of a planet, or as the body of you or of me.

It is utterly impossible for *anything* to be a solid mass. If there could be such a thing, God would have to be solidity. If God were solidity, God would have to be darkness because solidity would necessarily include darkness, or density. There is *no density* of darkness. There is only *intensity* of Light, *and God is Light.* The Light which is God—the Universe—is present in the *same* intensity throughout the Entirety which is God. Now you can see why there can be no solid bodies. You can understand why even the physicists maintain that matter is not the inactive, solid mass it appears to be.

Throughout the ages, it has been known that *God is Light.* Our Bible is replete with references to the Light, and this is also true of many other Bibles or religious works. Whether or not the fact that God is Light has been fully accepted, this fact remains: *God is Light.* Our own Bible states it plainly and emphatically: "This then is the message which we have heard of him, and declare unto you, that God is light, and in him is no darkness at all" (I John 1:5).

Yes, God is truly Light. Indeed, there is no darkness in the Light which is God. There is no solidity, no density, no materiality, and no matter existing in or as God. As we have said: God is the Universe. It is obvious that the Universe is Light and that in this Universe there is no darkness at all. There is *no such thing* as a body of solidity, whether this body be called star, planet, moon, or sun. Even if it should be called the body of you or of me, the fact remains: there are no bodies consisting of solidity, heaviness, or darkness.

Now you know the reason why there can be no solid, dark bodies. You can also see why *the Essence in form called body has to be comprised of Light.* So let us go on and discover just what comprises the Light which is the Essence of everybody in existence.

This is not all we are going to discover. We must perceive the nature of the activity of the Universe and the activity of each and every body constituting the completeness which is this Universe. To know the nature of this activity will not be sufficient unless we discover *why* the omnipresent Essence which is God is in constant action. This is an intelligent Universe. No one who observes the perfect order of the heavens can doubt this. If there is activity — and there is — there *must* be an intelligent purpose in this activity.

We have agreed that God is Mind, or Intelligence. If God is present in equal intensity throughout Its entirety, then Intelligence must be present in equal intensity throughout the entirety which is the Universe. It follows, then, that Intelligence must be present in and *as* equal intensity throughout the body of every star, every planet, the Earth planet.

This is the very same Intelligence that exists in equal intensity throughout your body and mine.

Conscious, living Intelligence is a universal fact. It exists everywhere and *equally* everywhere. We can even go farther than that. We can say that conscious, living Intelligence is the Everywhere. We know that God is indivisible. Thus, we know that conscious, living Intelligence is indivisible. We have discovered that this living Essence is not confined by the outline of the form in which It evidences Itself.

Now, let us clearly perceive the tremendous fact that *conscious, living Intelligence comprises the Essence and the Activity of the Universe.* This is why this is such a perfect Universe. This is why the activity which is evident in this Universe is such perfect activity. It could not be otherwise because It is infinite, perfect Mind in action. Intelligence acts intelligently; and intelligent activity is perfect activity. Perfect activity fulfills a perfect purpose; and Intelligence governs the activity and the purpose of the activity.

We know that Intelligence is enlightened Consciousness. Even in everyday conversation, we hear such expressions as "the Dark Ages," meaning a period in which Intelligence seemed to be missing— a period of ignorance. We hear an individual mentioned as being enlightened when he is thought to be exceedingly intelligent. Of course, these statements are symbolic because they refer to *assumptive* man. Yet they serve to point up the fact

93

that Intelligence is Light because God is Intelligence, and God is Light.

Enlightened Consciousness is intelligent Consciousness. Intelligent Consciousness is an active Consciousness. An intelligent, active Consciousness is a *living* Consciousness. This is true because activity is Life Itself. Without Life there could be no activity, and without activity there could be no Life. This Universe is comprised of intelligent, living Consciousness. This is enlightened, living Awareness, and this Awareness is Light.

That is why this is a Universe of Light. That is why many individuals have known that God is Light. That is why in complete illumination we are aware of such tremendous Light. Indeed, this Universe is Light, and in It *there is no darkness at all.* There are no dark spots called bodies of density in this Infinity we call the Universe.

It is of the utmost importance to accept the fact that *this Universe is God, fully aware of being Itself.*

That is a simple statement of fact, yet it is one of the most profound—if not *the* most profound—truths you can realize or know.

The Universe is a *living* Essence. This living Essence is a *conscious* Essence, for It is conscious Life Itself. This Universe is an intelligent Essence because conscious, living Intelligence constitutes Its entirety.

You will note that I have not mentioned the word *Love* in the foregoing. This omission does not mean that Love is not important. On the contrary, Love is of such vital importance that an entire chapter must be devoted to this dynamic aspect of the living Light. You may also have noted that the word *Principle* has not been used in the discussion of the Universe of Light. It seems apparent that the realization of Intelligence in action precludes the necessity for the word *Principle*. Intelligence is Omnipotence, and Omnipotence in intelligent action *is* Principle. Principle cannot deviate from being Itself because It is immutable by Its very nature.

We have said that this Universe is a living Essence. The activity of this living Essence is an intelligent, living activity. Furthermore, it is an *orderly* activity. The perfect order of universal activity is evident in the orderly way in which the heavenly bodies function. It is also apparent in the orbiting of our Earth planet, in the turning of the Earth on its axis. The coming and going of the tides, the seasons, etc., are evidence of the precise order in which this intelligent activity functions. Oh, there is precision in this orderly activity. Any deviation from this precision would not be Intelligence in action.

Now we have arrived at the important question: *What is the purpose of Intelligence in action?*

We know that God — the Universe — is eternal, without beginning, change, or ending. So there could be no *creative* purpose in this intelligent Omniaction. God is All, and God does not create, destroy, and recreate Itself. This would not be Intelligence in action. So there must be another purpose in this activity. There is. We know that God is a perfect God. We also know that God is Perfection. In order to be eternally perfect, Perfection must be maintained and sustained. It *is* maintained and sustained, and *that* is the purpose in the omniactive Intelligence we know to be evident. The infinite Essence which is God is *actively* maintaining Itself. Not only that—this infinite Intelligence is maintaining Itself *as* the perfection of Its infinite activity.

The purpose of Intelligence in action is the harmonious maintenance of this Universe in complete, uninterrupted perfection. If an interruption in this maintenance could take place, God—the Universe—would have to vacillate between perfection and imperfection. If there were periods of creation and destruction, God would have to create Itself, destroy Itself, and be engaged in a ceaseless cycle of Its own creation and destruction. This would not be Intelligence in action. Thus it is not God in action. If it is not God in action, it simply cannot be taking place, for there is nothing to act but God.

No one can deny that creation and destruction *appear* very real. Neither can it be denied that there is every appearance of inharmony, imperfection, and friction. We do not deny that there is apparent overwhelming evidence to the effect that the stars and planets do collide, deteriorate, and fall away from their orbits. This same appearance of the absence of God can be seen in airplane and automobile accidents and in every incident that does not reveal perfect, intelligent activity.

For that matter, there is apparently every evidence that objects and bodies seem to consist of solid masses of matter. Furthermore, there appears to be no evidence of the presence of activity in many of these deceptive masses of solidity. Yet leading physicists have discovered that this is *false* evidence. They have proved that matter—as it *appears*—does not exist. In fact, they have said that this appearance of solidity is energy. Yet they recognize that the activity of this "energy" is perfect, orderly activity. Thus even *their* experiments have proven that we cannot trust the evidence of the human mind or of human vision.

Now, what mind is it that knows anything about accidents? It makes no difference whether these accidents appear to be taking place in the heavens or on the streets of earth. The undependable illusory human mind is the *only* mind that can know them. The only vision that can see them is the vision of this same illusory man. And the only one who can recognize and report these non-intelligent accidents is the assumptive man of faulty human intelligence.

Being illusory by its very nature, it is inevitable that this illusory man will see, experience, and report the illusions of his own illusory nature. Yet even an illusion points up the fact that there is Something here to be deluded *about*. As stated before, there could be no illusion about nothing. The Something that does exist is God — the perfect Universe — in eternal, harmonious existence.

Assumptive man's mistaken concept of the Universe, the world, and the body can be compared to a mathematical mistake. No mistake could be made about the answer to any mathematical problem unless the correct answer did exist. No child would ask a teacher a question about mathematics — or anything else — unless he knew there was an answer to that question. The true answer to any question is the *perfect* answer.

> The true answer to any question about this Universe is that It is an eternally changeless, perfect Existent. This is the perfect answer.

If any evidence to the contrary appears to be present, it is *false* evidence — a mistake about the perfect Universe which does exist. This same fact holds true whether the false evidence is about the Universe, the heavenly bodies, the body of the Earth planet, or about your body or mine.

A perfect Universe must, of necessity, *act* perfectly. It does. Intelligence, God, in action is perfect Omniaction. This is the perfect answer to any question about the apparently imperfect activity of the Universe, the Earth, or the body.

An illusory concept of anything can see, experience, or produce only the evidence of the mistaken concept. This would be the case so long as the false evidence was believed to be true and genuine. Instantly the fact concerning anything is *known*, the mistaken concept vanishes. Thus, the mistake is corrected automatically. This correction is simultaneous with the true, or genuine, concept of that which the mistake was *about*.

This takes place every day among those who are engaged in discovering the genuine nature of the Universe, the world, and the body. When the true concept is revealed, they say they have experienced a healing. But have they? No. They have simply become aware of the mistake, and they have corrected it. Where have they corrected it? Right where it seemed to be true. How have they corrected it? By the conscious perception that there is no illusion—no mistake and no deluded one. In this perception, the seeming mistake has simply vanished.

Of course, in the fictional realm of illusion, it *is* possible for a fabled mortal to live an entire life span of illusions. It is also possible for innumerable mortals to experience the illusions of their own illusory nature. This is why the false evidence of imperfection appears to be so overwhelming. Yet the fact remains: God is eternal, infinite Perfection, and God is All. Thus, All is perfect.

No illusion can change this fact. No world mass of illusory evidence can change the fact that "there is one alone, and there is not a second; yea, he hath neither child nor brother" (Eccles. 4:8). Indeed, there is One alone. This One is the universal God who constitutes the *only* Universe in existence. There is no second universe. There is no second world. There is no second man or identity, and there is no second body of man.

There is never the necessity to change an illusion into the fact. This could never be done. It is necessary to perceive the fact, to know that which is true. No one can change an illusion into a more perfect illusion. This has been tried, but always there will be another imperfect illusion. In short, no matter how many healings one may see or experience, there is always going to be a need for further healing so long as the primary illusion persists. The primary illusion is that there is something existing that is not God. The primary fact is: God is All; All is God. It is as simple as that.

Whatever you know God to be, that are you and nothing else. If you do not know God to be what God *is*, you are still dwelling in mass illusion. You know what you are just to the extent that you do know what God is. And your entire Life, Mind, and experience will be the evidence of that which you know God to be.

You need not seek to change your Self, your world, or your Universe. It won't work. It can't be done. You can no more change your Self than you can change God, for God is your Self. For this same reason, you cannot change your world, your experience, or your Universe. God is your world, your experience, and your Universe. You can change nothing that is genuine. But you *can* discover what is real. You *can* recognize and accept enlightened Christ-Consciousness to be *your* Consciousness. In this way only are you going to *know* what God is. Only in this way are you going to know what *you* are, what the world is, and what constitutes your Universe. *What you know is what you are.*

It has been said that the Universe consists of God, conscious of being what It is. This same fact is true of you. All there is of you is what you know your Self to be. You cannot know what you are unless you know what God is, for God is All. When you do know what God is, you cannot help knowing what you are. You see, the *only* Mind that can know what God is, is the Mind that is God. "For what man knoweth the things of a man, save the spirit of man which is in him? even so the things of God knoweth no man, but the Spirit of God" (I Cor. 2:11).

Your Consciousness is your Universe. This is true because your Universe consists of just what you know. Furthermore, that which you are conscious of constitutes the entire essence and activity of your Universe. This is your answer to whether or not this Truth is a practical aid in your everyday living. Indeed it is. As you recognize, accept, and experience the universal fact that Perfection is All, you will discover that *your* daily life and experience is the evidence of this fact.

Does not the living Intelligence which governs Itself as the Universe also govern Itself as you? Does not this same living Mind govern your life, your activity, and your body? Indeed it does.

Let us proceed to discover how it is, and *why* it is, that your life, activity, and body are constantly governed and maintained by the infallible, universal Intelligence which is God.

We have discussed the fact that the Essence of the body of each star and planet consists of God. We realize that the body of everything in form is active. In fact, we know that there is intense activity going on throughout this entire Universe. This intense activity does not stop at the outline of the body of any star or planet. It is not excluded from the body of the sun or the moon. It continues to be the very same activity when it is evidenced as the intensely active Earth planet. Above all, this perfect activity does not cease to be active at the outline of *your* body.

One of the leading physicists has said that it is possible that the body does not generate or contain life and intelligence within itself. He infers that it is even probable that life and intelligence are elements of a universal nature that flow and surge *through* the body. Well, this physicist is coming close to the absolute fact. One day he will discover that living, conscious Mind is a universal Existent and that the body is comprised of this universal Existent. Then he will realize that intelligent, living Consciousness does not merely surge and flow *through* the body; he will perceive that it is the very Essence of which the body consists. He already knows, as do we, that living, conscious Mind is *not* confined within the outline of the body. We know why It is not confined. We know what the body really is. We perceive the *Body of Light*, which is the universal Light delineated.

Often we hear or read something to the effect that God governs this Universe. This is true, but it doesn't go far enough. God does not govern the bodies of the stars and planets in the way we drive a car or run a lawn mower. The heavenly bodies are not something *other* than God, to be governed by a power *outside* the substance of the bodies. God does not govern the activity of any body as a presence or power outside that body. God governs the essence of everybody in existence — *but God Itself is both the Essence and the Activity of that which is governed*. In short, God eternally and infinitely governs Itself and *only* Itself. How could it be otherwise when there is nothing other than God to be governed?

These bodies that appear to consist of solidity and darkness are not what they appear to be. Actually, they are *Bodies of Light*. This Universe is a Universe of Light. It can be nothing *but* Light because God is Light. The seeming darkness is not in the Universe. It is not in the heavenly bodies. It is not in the body of our planet, and it is not in the body of you or of me. In fact, it is not in the body of anything. It is not even in the body of a table, a chair, or an apple box. The seeming darkness is in the way *we* appear to see these bodies. It is in an illusory concept of an illusory man. Thus, the seeming darkness is not in any body; rather it *appears* to be in us so long as we apparently continue to "see through a glass, darkly" (I Cor. 13:12).

The illumined Christ-Consciousness dispels all apparent darkness and reveals the perfect Universe of Light. No longer do bodies appear dense and dark. No longer does life appear to be discordant and filled with problems to be solved. No longer does the body complain of pain, sickness, exhausttion, or depletion. No longer does the seemingly inevitable threat of old age and death constantly hang over our heads. We have realized the fulfillment of the promise "but when that which is perfect is come, then that which is in part shall be done away" (I Cor. 13:10). Yes, we can go even farther than that; we can say with conviction: "I know even as also I am known" (I Cor. 13:12).

Indeed we *do* know ourselves as we are known. God is the only One who knows anything. God knows only Itself. We are known of God, but it is *God knowing Itself.* Even our own consciousness that we exist is God knowing Itself.

> The only Self-Consciousness there is, is God conscious of being Itself. The only Self-knowledge there is, is God knowing Itself to be, and to be the eternal Perfection which It is.

Indeed, this is a Universe of Light. The Light is the all-intelligent Mind which is God. The Light is the all-living Life that is God. The Light is the enlightened Consciousness which is God. And this is your Intelligence; this is your Life; this is your Consciousness.

Furthermore, this universal Light is your *Body of Light:* the Body that was never born, can never change, and will never die.

The universal Light is the Christ-Consciousness which was evidenced as the One they called Jesus. It is the Christ-Consciousness of the One they call Mary, John, or whatever. In fact, it is the Christ-Consciousness of the One they call *you.*

Chapter VII

Love Is Light

It has been said that God is Love, and this is true. It has also been said that God is Light. This also is a statement of fact. This being true, it follows that Love is Light and Light is Love. Let us perceive in what way this universal Truth functions in the Universe, in the world, and in our daily affairs. Let us also see how the Love that is Light functions in and *as* our bodies.

Our first approach to *any* Truth should be from the universal standpoint. There are two primary reasons why this universal approach is advisable. First, whatever is an Existent in and as the Universe is an Existent in and as the life, body, and experience of the specific Identity. Second, when we consider any Truth from the standpoint of Its universality, we are released completely from any little personal sense of knowing, having, or being this universal Truth.

It is well to realize that it is the fallacious sense of a personal ego which seems to have all the trouble. *There is no personal Truth.* There is only the impersonal, universal, infinite Truth. Therefore, the only successful approach to any Truth must, of necessity, be from the point of view of Its universality.

Love is a universal Existent. It is a universal fact. It is present everywhere and equally everywhere. It is as omnipresent as is Life, Mind, Consciousness, or Light. Love is inseparable from conscious, living Mind. There is no place where Love leaves off and conscious, living Intelligence begins. They are one universal Existent, with no lines of demarcation between them. Wherever there is Consciousness, Life, or Intelligence, there is Love.

Obviously, we are not referring to human love. This temporary emotion called human love is indeed a sorry imitation of the infinite, omnipotent Love which is God. There is nothing temporary about infinite Love. It is an eternal Existent. Furthermore, it is an omnipresent fact of all Existence.

That which is called human love must have a beginning. Thus, it must also have an ending. It is subject to change, to fluctuation, and it can easily turn into its opposite, which is hate. Human love is possessive. It is often used as an excuse to dominate the so-called loved ones. There is no greater bondage than the chains of one who seems to be bound by human love.

How often we have seen someone struggle to free himself from the domination and restrictions of human love. Too often the one who loves in this mistaken way considers that he is the only one who must change. This is not true. It is as wrong to permit one's self to be dominated, or bound, as it is to dominate or enslave another with a false sense of love.

We have heard about the parent birds pushing the youngsters out of the nest when they were ready to fly. This is true. But there is another fact it would be well to consider. Once the young birds are independent of the parent birds, they remain independent. They do not keep right on flying back to have the parent bird feed them or to help them in any way. They have discovered that they are free, and this very freedom necessitates their own maintenance and self-sustenance. Thus, both the parent birds and the newly freed birds are completely free.

There is one more lesson in this example, namely, the young birds do not keep coming back to see how the parents are getting along. They feel no responsibility for the so-called old folks. They go on about their own affairs and permit the parents to do the same.

In order to be completely free from the bondage of human love, it is necessary to dissolve the chains *you* have forged around yourself. If you are still bound by your own false sense of love, how can you be free enough to help another to freedom? You can't. Never look to another for *your* freedom. Complete freedom must be realized by the individual himself. Actually, no one can free another. By this same token, no one can really bind another. Freedom is a private affair, and each one is responsible for his own freedom. No one can *give* freedom *to* another. Each one must realize his own freedom.

That which is called human love has within it the seeds of fear, hate, jealousy, domination, and human bondage. Human love engenders fear because there is always an inner realization that it is transitory. An assumptive human being believes that he can either receive or give love. He also believes that love can be given or withheld from him. He is always fearful of the loss, either of his loved one or of the love of his loved one. In either case, it is fear. No matter how happy one may be in one's love, there is an undercurrent of fear. Thus, it is never completely satisfying. More often than not, human love is a very frustrating experience.

Human love is an illusion. It is an illusion of assumptive man, who himself is part and parcel of the phantasmic world of illusion. It builds its own illusory images, then loves what it has built. It is always in bondage to its own fallacious nature. Being illusory by its very nature, its images and its emotions are necessarily delusions.

There is but *one* Love, and this Love is God. God does not consist of attributes. Therefore, Love is not an attribute of God. Rather it is God Itself. God does not give Love. Neither does God withhold Love. God cannot help loving because God cannot help *being* what God is. It is futile to appeal to God for Love. It is useless to expect God to show — or prove — His Love *for* you. The Love which is God is impersonal, and God can no more help loving than God can avoid *being* Love. God must ever be what God eternally *is*.

God is infinite, eternal Love. This Love must of necessity be completely impersonal. It never begins; It never wanes or fluctuates, and It can never come to an end. It is never interrupted by periods of fear, discord, jealousy, or hate. In the infinite Love which is God, there are *no* unloved ones. There can be no vacuums in omnipresent Love.

We have stated that Love and Intelligence are inseparable. If this be true—and it is—there can be no such thing as non-intelligent Love. Intelligence *must* fulfill an intelligent purpose. Thus, Intelligence must fulfill Its purpose in *being* Love. Yet Love must also fulfill Its purpose in being Intelligence. If intelligent Love did not fulfill Its purpose in being, God's infinite purpose would be only partially fulfilled. Thus, God Itself would be incomplete.

God comprises all that is necessary to His infinite, eternal completeness. Both Love and Intelligence are essential to this completeness. The presence of intelligent Love would be purposeless if It were not active. There is no fulfillment of any purpose without activity. God is Omniaction, and God's purpose is fulfilled through omniactive living, loving, conscious Intelligence.

Now let us perceive just *how* omniactive, intelligent Love functions as the fulfillment of this purpose. As always, our approach must be from the standpoint of the Universe. As we contemplate the heavens, we cannot help noting how beautifully perfect is the functioning of this Universe. Each galaxy is like a community of stars, planets, etc. Each galaxy is *that* specific galaxy and no other. There is no friction between one galaxy and another. Neither is there friction between one star or planet and another star or planet. Everything—galaxies, stars, and planets included—functions in perfect harmony.

There is a notable Oneness evidenced in the perfect activity of these heavenly bodies. This Oneness is Love, and the purpose of universal Love is the intelligent maintenance of the Universe in perfect harmony. The omniaction of universal, intelligent Love is the harmonious, intelligent activity which governs all Existence. It is active as the intelligent activity of each galaxy, each star, and each planet. It is active as the activity of our Earth planet. It is also active as your Life, your Consciousness, your daily experience, and your body.

There is no barrier to omniactive Love. The delineation which is called the form of your body does not bar universal Love from its own Essence. You see, Omniaction is not an activity that is isolated from Life, Consciousness, Intelligence. Rather Omniaction is the Love that is Life, Consciousness, Mind. Conscious, living, intelligent Love in action is Omniaction.

Conscious, living, intelligent Love is the Essence of each galaxy, each star, and each planet. This perfect Essence in action is Omniaction. Omniaction is God in action. God is Love, so Omniaction is Love in action. Love, being intelligent, acts perfectly. Mind, being Love, acts lovingly. In this way the purpose of universal Love is being fulfilled. There is no interruption of the fulfillment of this purpose, and there is no vacuum in which the intelligent purpose of universal Love is not being fulfilled.

Let us repeat:

> The purpose of universal Love is the perfect, eternal maintenance of all that constitutes the Universe.

We can take note of a simple example of this fact. Let us consider an ordinary pocket watch. Every item in the watch is necessary to its completeness. Furthermore, each item in the watch is exactly where it should be, doing just what it should be doing. No one part of the watch could function of itself. It would have no purpose in being if it were not necessary to the completeness of the watch. The activity of one part of the watch does not replace the activity of another part. For instance, the function of the mainspring does not take the place of the function of the balance wheel. One does not interfere with the other in the slightest degree. If there were any interference or friction, the perfect activity of the entire watch would be impaired; it might even be stopped. So the purpose of the activity of each part in the watch is the smooth, perfect functioning of the entire watch. If this were to fail, the watch itself would not fulfill its purpose.

The watch existed in and as the Consciousness of someone long before the so-called material watch ever appeared. In fact, we can truthfully say that the watch, including its perfect functioning, *always* existed. The assumed inventor simply discovered it. Certain it is that the Intelligence that discovered the principle of the watch always existed, and it was always complete. Thus, the activity of the watch had to be an eternal Existent.

As you know, any simile is inadequate. But the simile of the watch does help to point up the fact that Love is an eternal, infinite, essential aspect of God. It is essential for the harmonious activity of the Universe, for the intelligent activity of each star and planet. It is necessary for the perfect fulfillment of every purpose. In fact, it is necessary for the fulfillment of God's purpose in being you, your life, and your body.

It is Love that keeps everything in existence in perfect, peaceful harmony. It is Love that precludes the possibility of friction, displacement, usurpation, or clashing human wills. It is Love that makes accidents an impossibility. It is Love that functions as every event of your life and experience. This same Love is active as the activity of the entire Essence of each star and planet. It is the activity of the body of the Earth planet, and it is the activity of the entire Essence of your body and of mine.

You can see that there is nothing personal about infinite Love. But do not be deceived. Love is a living Essence. It is *alive.* It has to be alive, for It is Life Itself. It is not personal, but It certainly does function in and as the daily experience of each one of us. We could not live if this were not true. If it were possible for Love to be completely absent, there would be no Life existing as this Universe. Neither would there be Intelligence or Consciousness. Love is the radiance of the Light. Love is radiant Light. It is dynamic, intense, living, conscious *Intelligence in action.* And this is omniactive God.

"Love worketh no ill to his neighbor: therefore love is the fulfilling of the law" (Romans 13:10). Indeed, Love does fulfill the one and only law. Love fulfills the law of eternal, perfect Life—the law of infinite, conscious, living Intelligence. Omniactive Love is perfect fulfillment.

Love never criticizes. It knows nothing to criticize. It is always gentle, and It always speaks and acts with compassion and understanding. It is omnipotent—but oh, It is only the power of *being* Love Itself. It is impervious to offense; It is immune to seeming hatred, envy, or criticism. It knows only Itself, and It knows Itself to be Love.

The power of Love is Almighty. The activity of Love is the Almighty God in action. There is nothing in existence that can resist or obstruct infinite, impersonal Love. In fact, there is nothing in existence to interfere with the omnipotent, omnipresent, living Light which is Love.

There is no illumination so fraught with ecstasy as that in which the infinitude of Love is seen, known, and experienced. There is no revelation so fraught with the power of instantaneous Perfection as the revelation that all Existence is infinite, living Love.

Chapter VIII

The Omniactive Light

There is a word in our spiritual vocabulary that has received very little attention. This word is *Omniaction*. It seems very strange that more attention has not been focused upon this word because activity is always an important aspect of illumination. We have discussed Omniaction to some extent in previous chapters. However, this dynamic word is of such great importance that it is necessary to devote much more attention to its consideration.

As stated before, activity is an important aspect of illumination. Indeed it is important because without activity there could be no illumination. Consciousness must be vitally active, alive, in order to experience being illumined. A fully illumined Consciousness is an intensely alert Consciousness.

It is true that sometimes the velocity of this activity is so great that one *appears* to be in a tremendous void of stillness. Yet even in this experience, there is an inner awareness of dynamic, surging activity. One may compare this experience to a wheel that is turning at great speed. If the speed of the turning wheel is accelerated sufficiently, it appears to be immobile. If one judged by appearance, one would believe that the wheel was completely motionless.

Yet one would have an inner awareness that the wheel was turning at a great rate of speed. In the stillness of some aspects of illumination, there is this inner awareness that intense activity is taking place.

I know of no instance of illumination in which Existence is perceived to be completely static. On the contrary, in most moments of illumination there is an indescribable sense of activity. This wonderful sense of activity is the very basis of the ecstasy one experiences during illumination.

This is an active Universe. Its activity is so omnipresent that the only word which describes it is Omniaction. The word *Omniaction* — in common with so many other words in our spiritual vocabulary — denotes God. It is small wonder that this word is of such vital importance to every one of us. It is impossible to perceive or to realize the Allness which is God unless this Allness is known to be omniactive as well as omnipresent.

Omniaction means "everywhere active." But its meaning goes farther than this. It also denotes *equally active everywhere.* Omniaction is God, the Universe, in constant, uninterrupted action. There are no degrees of intensity in this activity. *It is present in equal intensity everywhere.* Because Omniaction is God, It is an infinite fact, or Truth. But God, the Universe, is eternal as well as infinite. Thus, Omniaction is an eternally infinite fact. God is the infinite, eternal Essence which comprises this Universe.

Omniaction is this infinite, eternal Essence in ceaseless, unwavering, immutable action.

There are no vacuums in Omniaction. It is indivisible, even as Life is indivisible, because It *is* Life. It is beginningless, changeless, endless. It is irrepressible, It is irresistible, and It is unobstructed. There is nothing in existence that can repress Omniaction. Neither is there anything which can resist or obstruct It.

Omniaction is as existent as is Life, Consciousness, Mind. We know that every star and planet is in constant motion. We know that our Earth planet is ceaselessly active. We know that this activity is not an activity which is excluded from the bodies of the stars and planets or from our earth body. The same Omniaction that functions as the orbiting of each star and planet is omniactive *throughout* the entire Essence of these bodies. This is also true of the body of our Earth planet.

Right now there is one point that must be clarified, and it must remain completely clear throughout our contemplation of the bodies of the stars and planets. It is exceedingly important that this point be clear in the perception of the body of our Earth planet. This point is: *the body of each star and planet, the body of our Earth planet, consists of Spirit, Consciousness, Intelligence, Life.* Thus, they are not comprised of solid or fluid masses of density or darkness.

Unless this point is clear, we are going to fall into the trap of materiality. God is All, and God cannot be the body of a mass of solidity, density, or darkness. With this point completely clear in Consciousness, let us proceed to discover the nature of universal activity—what it is and, above all, why it is such an important aspect of God.

We have clearly seen that Life, Intelligence, Consciousness are indivisibly One. We have also seen that the form of the body does not enclose or confine living, intelligent Consciousness. From our example of the light in the room, we have discovered that the conscious, living Mind which comprises the Universe exists as the Essence of the body.

Now let us perceive the way in which Omni-action fulfills Its vital purpose. As always, our first approach must be from the standpoint of the Universe. This universal activity is not excluded from the body of one single star or planet. It certainly is not excluded from our Earth planet. It is not a governing activity *outside* the body of our planet. Rather it is the very Essence of this planet in ceaseless, irresistible, unobstructed movement.

Sometimes we hear of God governing the movement of the stars and planets, as if God were performing His work from *outside* the bodies which He governs. Nothing could be farther from the truth. The activity that holds each planet in its proper orbit is equally active within and as the Essence of each heavenly or stellar body. There is no line of demarcation which divides Omniaction into separate little areas of activity. It cannot be blocked off into large or small blocks of Itself. It is one indivisible, surging, omnipresent, rhythmic activity, and it is the activity of the Essence of all form. Furthermore, *it is equally present*, whether it be the activity of the body of a planet or the activity of that which is called the atmosphere.

We have just mentioned the word *rhythmic*. This word is particularly important in what we are going to perceive, so it would be well to entertain it quite consistently in Consciousness. All activity is rhythmic in nature. Universal Omniaction is a universal, balanced, orderly, rhythmic movement. This perfect rhythmic activity is equally present, whether it is active as the body of the Universe, the body of a star, or the body of a grain of sand.

This is an orderly Universe, and all movement or activity of this Universe is a perfect, orderly, rhythmic activity. Intelligence in action is perfect, orderly, rhythmic activity. It has been said that all action is Mind in action, and this is true. Thus, all activity is intelligent activity. Intelligence in action does not act chaotically, non-intelligently, or destructively. It would not be intelligent for infinite Mind to act in a manner that would destroy Itself.

Within the infinite, surging, rhythmic Omniaction of the Universe are innumerable specific rhythms. Each rhythm is distinctly that rhythm, yet there is no dividing line between these rhythmic activities. There is rhythmic *distinction*, but there is no rhythmic *division*. No distinct rhythmic action can be divided or separated from the over-all universal, perfect, rhythmic Omniaction.

First, we have the surging, rhythmic activity of the entire Universe. Then we may consider the rhythms of the activities of the galaxies, the stars, the planets, and of our Earth planet. Let us, for a moment, consider the rhythmic Omniaction of our Earth planet. It is simultaneously active as three distinct rhythmic velocities. For instance, it is said to be rushing toward "the outer rim of space," revolving around the sun, and rotating upon its own axis. All of these specific rhythms are going on simultaneously as the activity of the Earth planet. It is noteworthy that each distinct activity is said to be taking place at its own specific rate of speed or velocity.

There is no way in which these three rhythmic activities can be separated. Neither is there a way in which the activity of the Earth planet can be separated from the universal Omniaction. We can continue this same concept throughout our Earth planet and the entire Universe.

Let us consider the coming and going of the tides. It is a well-known fact that the tides move in a precise, orderly, perfect rhythm. However, within this rhythm of the tides, there is the rhythm of the waves as they advance or recede. The rhythmic activity of each wave is inseparable from the activity of the tide itself. But this is not all. Within the rhythmic activity of each wave is the faster rhythm of each drop of water. Again, there can be no division between the rhythmic activity of the drop of water, the wave, and the tide. All of this is perfect, surging Omniaction, and it is all taking place simultaneously.

There are innumerable rhythmic activities going on right here and now. Furthermore, there are an *infinite variety* of distinct rhythmic activities. We have heard of the rhythm of the seasons. And in everyday experience we find countless rhythmic activities. We walk, talk, breathe, eat, and sleep in rhythmic patterns.

An interesting fact is the rhythmic surge of the cities. Each large metropolitan center has its own rhythm. On a recent visit to New York City, I occupied a room on one of the upper floors of a tall hotel. It was fascinating to stand before the open window and listen to the rhythmic, surging sound of the city. It could be compared to the perfect rhythm of a huge motor, and the sound seemed to ebb and flow as the sound of the ebbing and flowing of the tides.

When I descended to street level, I could discern countless rhythms *within* the over-all rhythm I had heard from the window of my room. For instance, I could hear the distinct rhythms of the motors in the automobiles and buses. Then there were the calls of the newsboys, sometimes like a rhythmic chant; the rhythm of walking; and sometimes the staccato clicking of high heels upon the sidewalks. Oh, there were countless distinct rhythms that were distinctly audible. While each and every activity in the city moves in its own rhythm, each activity is essentially the overall rhythmic activity of the city itself.

I have listened to the rhythm of many cities, and it is noteworthy that the overall rhythm of each city is distinctly *that* rhythm. For example, the rhythmic velocity of the city of New York is noticeably faster than is the rhythm of Los Angeles. The overall rhythm of San Francisco is somewhere between the rhythms of New York and Los Angeles. It has occurred to me that the rhythm of each city is essential to the overall rhythm of the entire nation; the rhythm of the nation is essential to the overall rhythm of the world; and the rhythm of the world — Earth planet — is essential to the overall rhythm of the Universe.

It is true that the foregoing is but a simile of that which is impossible to describe. Naturally, this simile is inadequate. But it does serve to point up the indivisible nature of the infinite, rhythmic activity that constantly surges and flows in and as the Universe.

We have mentioned rhythmic activity that can be seen and heard. But there is rhythmic activity of far greater importance. This is the activity that can be *sensed* but that is neither visible nor audible. This invisible, silent activity is Omniaction, or *God in constant action.*

There could be no activity unless there were *something* to act. There is; and this Something is God—the Universe. The Universe is an infinite Essence. There are some who say that It is a spiritual Universe, and they insist that Spirit constitutes its Essence. We do not quarrel with this statement, but unless we know what the word *Spirit* means, this word must have a very nebulous connotation. This is why the word *Consciousness* is of such great importance. The Universe is constituted of Consciousness, and Consciousness is conscious. Consciousness is the "Something" which is active. Consciousness is the Essence which is in constant, intelligent, rhythmic motion. Consciousness in action is the rhythmic activity which is *sensed,* and it is Consciousness which senses, or is aware of, this universal Omniaction.

Before we continue, let us be very clear about this word *Consciousness.* Sometimes the word is misunderstood. This misunderstanding stems from the illusion that there is a human consciousness. If there is no genuineness in a human being—and there isn't—there can be no human consciousness. Universal, omniactive Consciousness has nothing to do with a personal consciousness of assumptive man. It is indivisible; the constant activity of this Consciousness is inseparable. It is the so-called personal consciousness of assumptive man that is supposed to be separated into "consciousnesses." This is exactly why the assumptive "person" seems to have so much trouble. It always assumes it can do something or be something of itself, separate and apart from the All. Universal Consciousness is *never* separated. Certain it is that It could not be divided into innumerable little assumptive personal consciousnesses. The activity of omniactive Consciousness is never divided into the separate activities of innumerable little illusory personal consciousnesses.

Universal Consciousness is universal Awareness. To be conscious is to be aware.

The Essence of the Universe is Consciousness aware of being Itself. The activity of this Essence is Omniaction, or infinite Consciousness in action.

Omniactive Consciousness may be seen, heard, or sensed in illumination. When in illumination omniactive Consciousness is experienced, there is always an awareness of *being* that which is seen, heard, or sensed. In this experience, there is a tremendous awareness of the indivisible nature of the Universe. But the *glorious* aspect of illumination is a consciousness of *being* this inseparable Entirety.

The omniactive Consciousness which comprises the Universe is a living Essence. *This is a living Universe. It is alive.* There is nothing alive except Life. Life is activity. The activity of the living Essence — universal Consciousness — is infinite Life. We know that Life, Consciousness, Intelligence, Love are inseparably One. Thus, it is apparent that universal

Omniaction is living, conscious Intelligence in action. But of the utmost importance is the fact that Omniaction is conscious Love in action. In the chapter entitled "Love Is Light" we have stated that Love is essential to the perfect, harmonious fulfillment of the universal All. Now let us perceive the stupendous importance of *omniactive* Love, or Love in action.

God is Love; but God is Life. Thus, Love is Life. Do you see what this means? It means that Love is a living, acting Essence. It *has* to be a living Essence because It is inseparable from Consciousness, Intelligence, and Life. Omniactive Consciousness is Love in action. Love can only act lovingly. *Love is alive.* Isn't this a tremendous Truth? Indeed it is. You see, "God is love; and he that dwelleth in love dwelleth in God, and God in him" (I John 4:16). The living Love which is God is *alive* as the omniactive, conscious Mind which is God. *You are alive. You are conscious.* You are loving and you are intelligent.

Oh, can't you see that *Love is your very Life,* your Consciousness, your Mind? The activity of the Love you are is Life Itself in action. This is why your entire experience is so beautifully harmonious and perfect. This is why your entire activity is so satisfying and effortless. This is why your entire Life, Consciousness, being, and body are so perfect and *act so perfectly.*

Is it any wonder that the enlightened one called John could say, "There is no fear in love; but perfect love casteth out fear: because fear hath torment. He that feareth is not made perfect in love" (I John 4:18). Perfect Love is perfect Life, and *this is your Life.* How can fear exist in a Consciousness which is aware of being perfect, living, conscious Intelligence? It cannot. It does not. What is there to fear? Who is it that fears? Fear is unknown to the Mind which is God.

Fear would claim to be the activity of an assumptive human mind. If such a mind could exist, it would be subject to fear because it could know nothing of itself. The assumptive mind of man fears the unknown. This very fear is manifested as skepticism, even suspicion, of the unknown. But this is not all. If there could be anything opposite to Love, it would be fear, for fear and hate are identical illusions. The phantasmic mind of man hates what it fears, and fears what it hates. Love in action is the activity of infinite Consciousness, Intelligence. There is no fear in Love because there is no fear in conscious, living Intelligence.

It is necessary to recognize that infinite, rhythmic, surging Omniaction is Love in action. If ever there were anything in need of healing, this realization would instantaneously heal it. As there is nothing in need of healing, the realization of *being* perfect, living, conscious Love in action reveals the presence of Perfection. This perfect, living, loving, intelligent Consciousness is alive and active this very moment as your Life, your affairs, your home, your experience, and your body.

Life, Consciousness, Intelligence, Love constitute the entire Essence of the Universe. The activity of this Essence is Omniaction, or omnipresent activity. An assumptive human mind never recognizes, sees, hears, or knows this Essence or Its activity. But It certainly is seen, heard, recognized, and known by the conscious, living Intelligence which *you* are. There is scriptural authority for the statement that no mythical "man with breath in his nostrils" shall see or know God. "And he said, Thou canst not see my face: for there shall no man see me, and live" (Exodus 33:20).

God *can* be seen, heard, known, and experienced. But no assumptive personal man can see, hear, know, or experience God. It is only the illumined Christ-Consciousness which can be aware of God. Jesus was well aware of this fact. Before he disappeared from the view of "worldly men," he said to the disciples, "Yet a little while, and the world seeth me no more; but ye see me: because I live, ye shall live also" (John 14: 19).

The fallacious appearance called man can no more see the illumined Christ-Identity than it can see God. Assumptive life is not Life. Assumptive mind, consciousness, love are not conscious, living, loving Intelligence. Assumptive man cannot see the Essence or the activity of the Essence which is living, conscious Mind. It takes the illumined Christ-Consciousness to see, know, or experience being that Life, Mind, Consciousness, Love which is God.

Jesus felt that the disciples were sufficiently illumined to "see" him as he was, and is. He knew that if they saw his Body of Light, they would see Life Itself. Furthermore, he knew that to *see* Life is to *be* Life. This is what he meant when he said that because the disciples saw him, they would live.

Now we have arrived at the point where it is necessary to clarify further the living Light which comprises the Universe. When, in illumination, we are seeing and being this omniactive Light, just what are we seeing, and what are we being? The answer to this question will, if understood, be evidenced as the illumined Christ-Consciousness. So let us proceed to inquire further into that which comprises this living, active, radiant Universe.

When, in illumination, you are aware of seeing and being radiant, universal Light, you are aware of seeing and being the very presence of God. No one who has this experience can go on seeming to live as a selfish, personal mortal. No wonder the Bible states that no man shall see the face of God and live. When one lives as an illumined being, it is impossible even to appear to live as a selfish little human life.

As we have stated, the universal Light is an intensely active Essence. Everyone who experiences illumination knows this to be true. The universal Light is pure Radiance. But Radiance must radiate, and the radiation of Radiance is Omniaction, or intelligent, living, loving Consciousness, in action.

The active radiation of Radiance is the surging, rhythmical, irrepressible activity of this entire Universe. In short, it is the Universe in ceaseless, irresistible motion. Without rhythm, there would be no order in this universal activity. But there is order, for this is an intelligent, orderly Universe. The radiation of the universal Radiance is the activity of each star and planet. It is the activity of the planet Earth. It is the activity of the infinite Essence in or as any form. But this is not all. It is the activity of what is called the atmosphere — the universal Presence which is said to be uninhabited space. Omniactive Radiance radiates universally. It radiates in equal intensity everywhere, and there is no smallest point where It is not in complete radiation. Neither is there a moment in which this universal Radiance is not complete as Its own radiance.

The radiant Infinite is the infinitesimal, radiating *as* the living Light. There is no greater or lesser Radiance. Neither is there greater or lesser radiation. There is distinction of rhythm, but there is no separation of the universal radiation. Neither is there any greater or lesser Intelligence, Life, Love, Consciousness in that Essence which is radiating.

The irrepressible surge and flow of Light may be compared to an infinite, universal tide. Within the irresistible flow of this universal, rhythmic Omniaction are countless rhythmic impulses in ceaseless, uninterrupted activity. Even as the rhythm of the drop of water in the tide is distinctly *that* specific rhythm and the rhythm of the wave is distinctly *that* rhythm—yet they are inseparably one— so it is that the numberless rhythms of the Universe are inseparable from the infinite, universal, rhythmic Omniaction. It is all one intelligent, rhythmic, orderly Omniaction. It is infinite in nature yet specific. The specific is the Infinite, even as the Infinite is the specific.

Illumined Consciousness is the Essence of the Radiance you see when you are in illumination. But *you* have to be illumined Consciousness in order to see this radiant Universe. So the Radiance you see is your own illumined Consciousness. That is why you always have a tremendous sense of being the Radiance you are seeing. You *are* the Radiance Itself.

The radiation of the Radiance you see is the Life that is conscious of being alive. But *you* are alive, so the activity of the Light is your very Life. This is why you can never be separated from your Life. *Life is what you are.* The surging, flowing Omniaction which is Life is *alive* as *your* eternal, immutable Life, right here and now. This omniactive, radiating Light does not stop at the outline of your body. It is inseparable from the Essence of your body. You see, Consciousness, Mind, Life, Love are indivisible.

You will recall an earlier reference to the discoveries by Sir Arthur Eddington, a renowned physicist. He says, in essence, that something takes place between the seeing of an object and the object itself which changes its appearance. Experiments have proven—beyond doubt—that there is intense activity taking place right where an appearance of solid matter presents a picture of inactive solidity. He describes it as being somewhat like innumerable little gnats scurrying around. Sir Arthur Eddington, a truly great physicist, was right at the standpoint of the great discovery that Life is omnipresent. It *is* omnipresent, you know, because Life is Omniaction. That which is alive is illumined Consciousness living, moving, and having Its being as the entire Essence of the Universe, the body of the Earth, the body of you and of me.

As stated in a previous chapter, it has been believed that life enters the body and that thereafter the body continues to generate life. This is also considered to be true of Consciousness and Intelligence, or Mind. You are not a center from which Life radiates. You are conscious, intelligent, radiant Life Itself. The radiant Life you are will seem to be more or less apparent according to the intensity of your consciousness of *being* the Light. You are the Light, and you are radiant as this Life.

In other words, you radiate Light, but you do not *generate* Light. You are the Light, and the Light is Its own radiation. You are not a center from which the Light radiates. It is well to remind yourself that the living Light you are is present in equal intensity throughout and as Infinity. There can be no boundary for the Light you are because It is boundless, spaceless, timeless, immeasurable, and limitless.

Omniaction is a universal fact. A universal fact is true everywhere, and it is equally true everywhere. Universal Omniaction is the activity that is taking place in and as your bodily activity this instant. This statement has been made here before, and although I do not wish to be repetitious, it is well to restate this Truth just at this point, as a foundation for what is to follow.

As previously stated, there is a growing conviction among leading physicists that the activity of the body stems from rhythmic impulsions from the Universe. It is also recognized that this activity is rhythmic in its nature. They have experimented with oysters, snails, and even with various vegetables. Their experiments have convinced them that everything moves in and as the same rhythmic activity which takes place in what they call outer space.

Of course, these studies and experiments are conducted from the standpoint of what is termed "matter." Yet they recognize the fact that matter as such does not exist. The physicists who are investigating the rhythmic patterns of activity call the impulses of these rhythms "electromagnetic fields," or "electricity in the air." It is wonderful to realize that even those who believe so firmly in a world of materiality are beginning to perceive that universal Omniaction is the *only* activity of the body, of a planet, of a carrot, or of you or me.

One thing is exceedingly clear: the whole world is on the way to the discovery that conscious, living, loving Intelligence is not confined to the body, and neither does the body generate conscious, living Mind within itself. Furthermore, that which the physicists are laboring to discover, *we already know because we experience illumination.*

In line with this fact, it is noteworthy that years before the physicists discovered that matter did not exist, a great illumined individual made the flat statement, "There is no matter." She knew this to be true because she was illumined. The physicists are still discovering more about the living, conscious Mind, although this Mind is very well known by all illumined beings.

This leads to the realization of one all-important fact: the *only* activity in existence is universal Omniaction, and nothing acts of itself, separate from or apart from the one all-infinite Omniaction. It makes no difference whether the activity is that of a planet or the activity of a so-called cell of the body, it is inseparable from universal Omniaction. Furthermore, there is no activity that is not an orderly, surging, rhythmic movement.

If you have read thus far in this book, you are now aware of the indivisible Universe which we call God. You are also cognizant of the fact that you exist *only* because this perfect, rhythmic, universal, omniactive All constitutes your entire life, being, experience, and body. The statements of Truth you have been reading are irrefutable facts. But it is not enough for you unless these facts are apparent in your daily affairs, in your life, and in your body. In other words, the evidence of any fact is necessary if you are to realize fully that any Truth is absolutely true.

If you have fully accepted the universal facts you have been reading, you are now prepared to perceive how it is, and why it is, that these facts can be evidenced in your everyday affairs. But this is not all; you are now ready to perceive why these facts have *not* been apparent or evident in your daily experience and in your bodily experience.

The way for this specific realization has been prepared. This has been done through the banishment of all fictitious boundaries and your own revelation that you are eternal, living, loving, conscious Mind *through and through*. Our next chapter will be devoted to perceiving and experiencing the *evidence* of the universal facts we have stated.

Chapter IX

The Evidence

Illumination is not an experience that has just recently come into being. Throughout the ages there have been illumined ones. Yet these greatly illumined ones have apparently continued to have sick bodies and to die. From this it would seem that what they perceived as illumined beings was not evident in their daily lives and experiences. If *we* are to experience the evidence of that which we perceive in illumination, we must realize that our illumined experience is our *entire* existence. We cannot accept one iota of anything which appears to be the opposite of, or different from, the glorious Universe which is so vividly apparent in illumination.

Any fact should be capable of proof. The evidence of any fact is the proof that it is true. If the evidence of a fact be missing, it can mean only that there is some misconception or some mistake about the fact. Let us examine a simple example of the Truth we have just stated.

The number 3 has always symbolized completeness. It appears repeatedly in the Bible, and it also appears in the religious writings of the East. You will note that Jesus mentioned three days as the symbolic figure for the length of time it would take for him to raise his body from the sepulchre. When Jesus went up to the Mount of Transfiguration, he was accompanied by three disciples—Peter, James, and John. It has always seemed significant to me that the event of the Transfiguration involved three fully illumined beings and three who were apparently not yet fully illumined. Jesus, Moses, and Elias (Elijah) were certainly illumined. Apparently Peter, James, and John experienced *some* illumination during that event. There are numerous other references to the number 3 in the Bible, but this will suffice to clarify our point.

The point we wish to make right now is that completeness is a universal fact. God is this Universe and God is complete. Thus, this is a complete Universe. God is Eternality, so the completeness which is this Universe is an eternal fact. However, this eternal, universal fact may not appear to be manifested in your experience if any aspect of its completeness appears to be absent.

Let us consider Perfection for a moment. God is eternal Perfection and God is the Universe. Thus, eternal Perfection is a universal fact. But Perfection must be *completely* perfect if It is to be Perfection at all. If there were the slightest flaw or disorder in Perfection, It would not be completely perfect; thus, It could not be called Perfection. So completeness is essential to the Perfection of that which is perfect.

Perfection is omnipresent as well as being omni-active. However, if you are not aware of this fact, it will not be apparent in your daily experience. So now we have stated two aspects of the completeness which is necessary to Perfection, namely the universal fact—complete Perfection—and *your consciousness* of this fact. The third aspect of this universal fact is also necessary if it is to be fully apparent in and as your daily experience and as your bodily experience. This third aspect is the *evidence, or manifestation, of the universal fact—complete Perfection.*

You know that the universal fact exists. You can know of its existence only because you are conscious. Consciousness is the Essence of all Existence, and Consciousness is always actively being conscious. Consciousness is the Essence of complete Perfection, and Consciousness in action is the recognition of this universal fact.

> Your Consciousness, actively aware of omni-present Perfection, is the Essence and the activity of that which It perceives. Thus, the evidence— manifestation—of complete Perfection is consti-tuted of your own Consciousness.

Here we have an example of the completeness of the universal fact—complete Perfection. Further-more, we have perceived the additional fact that you are inseparable from the *evidence* of the Perfection you have perceived. You are never separated from your own Consciousness and Its activity.

Let us now clarify this by a simple illustration. It is a mathematical fact that $2 + 2 = 4$. This is a universal fact because it is true throughout the entire

Universe. Furthermore, it is an eternal fact because it never began and it can never come to an end. Although this universal fact has existed universally and eternally, it would appear that *you* have not always been aware of its existence. In other words, it seems that you had to learn of its existence before it could be a fact in and as your experience. Once you are aware of this fact, you may see the evidence of its existence at any moment or anywhere. All that is necessary for the evidence to be apparent is that you focus your attention upon the existing fact.

The universal fact is within your Consciousness, so it *is* your Consciousness. When your attention is focused upon this specific fact, your Consciousness is actively aware of its existence. Thus, its existence is evident to you. It is more than evident *to* you. The evidence of the universal fact exists within and *as* your own Consciousness. So the evidence is comprised of your own Consciousness.

This is an example of the fact that the universal (infinite) fact is the specific (infinitesimal) fact. It is also true that the specific (infinitesimal) fact is the universal (infinite) fact. Wherever and whenever the fact exists, the evidence of this fact can be perceived at any moment. The fact is the universal Principle. The evidence is the manifestation of the perfect Principle as the experience of anyone who consciously perceives the universal perfect Principle.

The Principle, or fact, of anything must always be approached from the standpoint of Its universality.

This is true because any Truth is a universal Truth. It is a mistake to approach any fact from the standpoint of the infinitesimal, or the evidence. Too often we have looked for the evidence first, then attempted to make this evidence *become* true in our own little affairs. We have attempted to approach universal Perfection from the standpoint of the manifestation, and then we have tried to force Consciousness into being aware of the perfect evidence.

We should have approached Perfection from the standpoint of the Completeness which is universal Perfection. In this way, we can be sure that our approach is impersonal. Perfection is an impersonal fact. It belongs to no one. It simply *is*. If we attempt to personalize It, we are attempting to divide the indivisible God. Furthermore, we are trying to minimize the immeasurable Infinite One.

There is no imperfect fact. The fact is the Principle, and the Principle is *always* perfect. The perfect, universal fact *is all there is*. There is nothing existing that is not the perfect universal fact.

You are the universal Consciousness. Thus, you are the universal perfect fact. You can never claim to be the universal perfect fact as a person.

> Only the Consciousness which is God can claim to be God. If you are fully aware that you are the impersonal perfect fact—Truth—you can truthfully, and with humility, say: I am the Truth. I am the universal perfect fact.

Your inseparability from the evidence of complete Perfection depends entirely upon your impersonal recognition of the fact that of yourself you are nothing. It seems a paradox that only through the acceptance of the fact that you, as a person, are nothing can you fully realize that you are Something. Only in this way can you perceive that you are the Something which is this entire, completely perfect Universe.

So long as you are inordinately concerned about the evidence of perfection in your daily experience, you are seemingly separating yourself from the indivisible, complete Perfection which constitutes the Universe. It is not until the little false personal ego is obliterated that the full power of the complete, universal Perfection can be realized and evidenced.

Once you have perceived that you are the impersonal, universal, complete Perfection, the evidence is inevitable.

This is true because the evidence consists of the Consciousness you are, aware of *being* what you are.

Once the little false, egotistical concept of self is banished, you need have no hesitancy in saying: I am that I AM. It makes no difference how severe may seem to be the problem, the universal perfect Truth that I am is all that is present. Furthermore, the universal perfect fact that I am is all that I can know to be present. I know what I am, and I know nothing else. I am what I know, and I am nothing else. Therefore, I can and do focus my attention *only* upon the perfect, complete, universal fact which I am.

In complete realization of being the perfect fact, you can confidently say:

> I am the perfect fact. I am conscious of being the perfect fact, and the Consciousness I am is the Essence and the activity of the perfect fact I am. This is completeness. This is complete Perfection, and this is the evidence of complete Perfection.
>
> I am the fact that all Substance is eternal and immutably perfect. I am the fact that all Substance is imperishable, indestructible.
>
> I am the fact that all Existence is ever new and that all Existence is inexhaustible and not subject to depletion. I am the fact that all Existence is Life, Consciousness, Intelligence, Love.
>
> I am the fact that all Substance is Light and not darkness. I am the fact that all activity is Omniaction, or perfect God in action.

In this way, you have banished any fallacious sense of being a little egotistical person. You have also impersonalized any seeming problem. You have dismissed that which seemed to be the problem, and you have dismissed the illusion that there is a person having—or aware of having—a problem.

Once the assumptive ego is obliterated, you can be assured that you are perceiving everything from the universal standpoint. This means that you are seeing as God sees and knowing as God knows. It is in this universal awareness that you can say, "I am impervious to any personal sense of being, for I am that I AM. I am my own immunity to inharmony of any kind, for I am the universal perfect Truth."

If Jesus had not known this to be true, he would never have said, "I am the way, the truth, and the life: no man cometh unto the Father, but by me" (John 14:6). Yes, the universal Christ-Consciousness is the way, and no one can perceive that God is the entirety of one's existence unless one realizes that one *is* the Truth. By the recognition that one is the Truth, the Identity perceives one's universal, perfect, changeless nature.

Let us, for a moment, return to our mathematical simile. If you are conscious of the fact that $2 + 2 = 4$, you can perceive the evidence of this fact at any moment of the day or night. You are aware that this fact exists wherever you are, and it exists whether or not your attention is focused upon it. But if, for any reason, this fact were essential to your perfect knowledge or activity at any given moment, your attention would immediately be focused upon it. Thus, you are *actively* aware of this specific fact; your omniactive Consciousness is actively engaged in the perception of this particular fact.

All that is necessary, as far as you are concerned, is that you focus your attention upon the perfect fact. Instantly as your attention is focused upon this fact, it becomes an *evident* fact in your experience. You may read it, you may speak it, you may write it or signify it in innumerable ways. The point is that you can see and experience the evidence of any specific fact simultaneously with the focusing of your attention upon it.

This is the wonderful thing about the realization that you are universal, conscious, living Mind. The instantaneity of omnipresent Perfection is often called "instantaneous healing." But is it healing? Indeed it is not. What is called instantaneous healing is but the sudden revelation of the evidence. This evidence has always existed but has suddenly been revealed. And it is revealed the very instant your universal Consciousness is focused upon it. Then you can joyously say, "The universal eternal Perfection is manifested (evident) as the I AM that I am."

The evidence is not the primary aspect of perfection to be considered. The perfect Principle is of vital importance. The perfect Principle is the universal fact. Once the perfect fact is known and attention is focused upon it, the evidence is inevitable.

Does this seem impossible? Well, it isn't. It is being proved every day, and it is beyond questioning or doubt. Oh, this is a practical Truth. It proves Itself to be true as our daily experience and as the health of our bodies. If It were merely a beautiful theory, there would be no proof of Its rightness or of Its universality. But if this Truth is to be evident in and as the daily experience of the student, there must be complete abandonment of an assumptive ego. I cannot stress too strongly the importance of obliterating the fallacious sense of a little personal self.

Let us now perceive just *why* it is vitally important to completely banish the assumptive little ego self—the little "I." First of all, the little "I" is but a pretense. Having no genuine existence, it can appear only to pretend to be something of itself. Because it pretends to be something of itself, it also imagines that it can do something of itself. It would, if possible, usurp the infinite Identity and supplant itself as omnipresent Omnipotence. Some of us have even seen and heard it strutting around saying, "I am God."

Nothing could be more ridiculous. Nothing could be farther from the truth. *God alone is God, and there is none other.* No little assumptive "I," believing itself to be something of itself, can claim to be God. God speaks *only* when there is no little "I" around trying to talk. *And when God speaks, there is no ego.* "There is one alone, and there is not a second; yea, he hath neither child nor brother" (Eccles. 4:8).

The assumptive little "I" would attempt to enthrone itself, to establish its own kingdom and govern of itself. It would attempt to rule itself—and everyone else, if it could—as if it were omnipotent. It appears as human ambition, selfishness, avarice, egotism, and innumerable other fallacious aspects of its pretense. It can even pretend to be the head of some great government, enslaving its people. Being limited by its very nature, it would limit everyone and everything it seemed to control. It is unnecessary to go any farther with the fallacious pretenses of the little "I." We know too much about these pretensions already.

But let us perceive just *why* this assumptive man must be obliterated. So long as it seems genuine, it can appear to interfere with the perception of omni-active, conscious, living Intelligence. So long as it seems to imagine that it can do something of itself, it will appear to be in the way of the infinite, rhythmic Omniaction. In fact, it can even appear to act *in opposition* to omnipotent Omniaction. And right here is where it gets into trouble. It struggles and frets. It strains for success. Its activity is labored and difficult. It seems always to be trying to swim against the current, and it finally has to relinquish all its efforts. This relinquishment is inevitable, because the little assumptive "I" is temporal by its very fictitious nature.

The wave might as well try to stem the tide as for one to attempt to act of one's self and in opposition to infinite Omniaction. Suppose the drop of water insisted upon going in the wrong direction. Suppose it tried to act of itself, apart from and in opposition to the tide. How far would it go? Not very far. And neither can little assumptive man get very far by trying to do something or to be something of itself. Furthermore, even that which appears to be success is accomplished with great sacrifice, labor, and struggle.

In contradistinction to all of this, Jesus said, "Take my yoke upon you, and learn of me; for I am meek and lowly in heart: and ye shall find rest unto your souls. For my yoke is easy, and my burden is light" (Matt. 11:29, 30). Indeed, Jesus *was* meek and humble. In his Heart-Consciousness—he knew that of himself he was nothing. He knew that he could have *no* existence unless it was God existing. He knew that he could not act of himself, separate or apart from the one infinite Omniaction. He was not bound with a heavy yoke of limitation. Neither was he burdened with a fallacious sense of self-importance. He could, and did, act without labor, worry, struggle, or strain. You see, he did nothing of himself. He knew it was infinite Omniaction consciously fulfilling Itself as his activity.

Jesus has been called "the man of sorrows," but I cannot accept this description of the enlightened Christ-Consciousness. I am convinced that he was exceedingly joyous and that nothing could diminish his joy. He was illumined, and who, in illumination, is sorrowful? Omniaction is joyous activity. Omniaction is effortless activity. It is without strain, worry, uncertainty, or struggle. It is limitless in terms of assumptive time and space. It is never interrupted, and it can never come to an end. Oh, if there were only words with which to tell you the dynamic joy of working because God is active as your activity. Of course, many of you are already aware of this joy. You know it cannot be described, but you know it to be pure, unlabored ecstasy.

Is it an effort for Life to be alive? Is it a struggle for Consciousness to be conscious? Is it a strain for Mind to be intelligent? And is it difficult for Love to be loving? No! No! No! *Neither is it a struggle for you to be what you already are.* The only reason there even *appears* to be a struggle is that there seems to be a little assumptive man to struggle. But the appearance is not you. The appearance is not your genuine and only Identity. The appearance is just what the word denotes—appearance—and nothing else. And when your illumined Christ-Consciousness reveals Itself to be your Self, there can no longer be even an appearance of a little assumptive "I."

A few words of caution should be stated right now. In the process of recognizing your freedom from the little "I," be sure that you do not honor it. Don't make something of nothing. Don't make an *effort* to rid yourself of something which has no existence in or as your Identity. Sometimes one will try so hard to rid one's self of an assumptive identity that one will only temporarily submerge it, and it will seem to spring forth in another guise, perhaps more seemingly violent and aggressive than ever.

Is it an effort for you to know that you are conscious, that you are alive, and that you are intelligent and loving? Is it an effort for you to *be* conscious, alive, intelligent, and loving? No! It is never a matter of getting rid of a pretense. It is always a matter of knowing so well what you *are* that the pretense just disappears naturally without any effort at all.

Knowing what you genuinely are precludes the necessity for affirmations and denials. An assumptive little "I" does not vanish through the denial that it exists. Neither does it help to affirm that it must disappear. No mental gymnastics will dismiss the illusion called a little "I." No concentrated mental effort will obliterate it. Never set up a straw man and then try to use it for target practice, hoping that in some way it will miraculously vanish. It won't disappear, you know, because you are watching it; you are too conscious of it.

Once it is banished completely, you realize that you have banished nothing. You are completely aware of that which does exist, and there is nothing else. You realize that never was there anything other than the complete, perfect, radiant, living Existence which constitutes this Universe. And this is *you*. This is all there is of you. In other words, the evidence of that which does exist is so complete and so apparent that you are unaware of any spurious evidence. "But when that which is perfect is come, then that which is in part shall be done away" (I Cor. 13:10). Yes, "that which is in part" is obliterated. Knowing the genuine I AM that you are simply cancels the little presumptuous self. It never was anything, and you never knew it to be anything.

Because you are infinite, you are everywhere. You are everywhere because you are the Everywhere. Wherever your attention is focused, there are you. Whenever your attention is focused, then are you. In this way, you realize that "there" is "here" to you. In this same way, it is apparent that "then" is "now." You are centered everywhere, but you are without circumference. For instance, right now my attention may be focused in New York City, even though I am at home in Vista, California. Where my attention is focused, there am I. But because I am there, "there" is "here" as far as I am concerned.

In like manner, my attention may be called to something that seemed to take place in what is called the past, although there is no past or future. Nevertheless, if I am considering something that was supposed to have taken place last year, or a hundred years ago, this supposedly past event is right now within my Consciousness. So the so-called past in which it happened is *now* to me. If I supposedly "look ahead" a day, a month, a year, or a hundred years, the seeming future is within my Consciousness *now;* so it—the future—is "now" to me.

Thus, it is apparent that there is no time and there is no space. There is only here and now. Full, complete, unconditional, unqualified Perfection is here, now. The full, complete evidence of infinite Perfection is right here and right now.

You have never been, and will never be, any more perfect than you are right now.

You are not victimized by a human past or by an uncertain future. If a seeming problem should appear in your experience, you do not attempt to do something about the problem. Neither do you ignore it. Something has taken place that has attracted your attention at the moment. Thus, your attention is focused upon some specific aspect of Existence. You cannot bury your head in the sand and just pretend that it will go away if you don't look at it. This would not be intelligent; thus, it would not be Intelligence in action. The omnipresent Mind you are is omniactive, so It must always act intelligently.

Now, you may very well be questioning something like this: If I cannot do anything about a problem, and I cannot ignore it, what is the right way to banish the problem?

There is a way to realize your complete freedom from *any* difficulty. It makes no difference how severe it may seem to be or how long it may appear to have been in your experience. Indeed, there is a way, but the way is not one of mental treatments. It is not the way of a method or of a formula. The way is an illumined way. It is the way of illumined seeing and being.

I cannot give you a method of procedure for this glorious experience. Illumination is a private affair. And no one can tell you how to bring about this experience. No one can have the experience *for* you, and no one can really explain it to you. I can tell you what constitutes your Existence. But *you alone must discover why you are what you are.* The *why* must be a revelation of your own Consciousness.

You see, it is only when you consciously experience being what you eternally are that you can know *why* you are *what* you are. In the following chapter, I shall share with you the way, or ways, that have been most helpful in my experience and in the experience of many others. Even so, you will realize that no words or combination of words can act as a formula by which illumination may be induced. It simply cannot be done through the use of methods or formulas. The way of illumination is to perceive that you are the Light radiating as Its own Radiance. You are the Light. You are the Radiance. You are the one who must be conscious of being what you eternally and infinitely are.

As you read the chapter that follows, it would be well for you to consider some facts pertaining to your Self. For instance, consider the Intelligence that you are—complete, infinite. Then you will perceive that what you are going to read already exists in and as your own Consciousness. It will not be new to you. In fact, you will probably realize that somehow you have always known it. Indeed you have known it—and will know it—throughout the infinity and eternity of your entire being. So do not approach the Truths presented in the following pages as if they were entirely new to you. Rather, approach them in the full realization that you already know them. You are just reminding yourself of that which you already know. In fact, you may even realize that you knew every Truth presented in this book, even as it was being written—or better still, *before it* was written.

Now, as full, open Consciousness, let us continue in our exploration of the infinite All which constitutes our entire Life, Mind, Being, and Body.

Chapter X

The Perfect Answer

Full illumined Consciousness is the goal of every dedicated student of Truth. This important goal becomes more and more important as our search continues. Sometimes the way *seems* long, and even arduous, and many obstacles seem to appear in our path. Yet we continue on, knowing inherently that illumination reveals the answer to every question we have ever asked and the solution to every seeming problem that has ever appeared.

This goal is reached when we fully realize that God is All, All is God. In this realization, we must go all the way. There can be no qualification and no degree in our acceptance of this basic fact. The complete acceptance of the Allness that is God precludes the recognition of anything that is *not* God.

For most of us, it is not difficult to accept the statement "God is All." Somehow we know this to be true. Even so, there are many questions that seem, for a while, to be unanswered. So long as we are not aware of the answers to these questions, they can *appear* to act as deterrents to our full realization of full illumination. We discover that the answer to every question already exists within and as our own

Consciousness. We also discover that the question, of itself, is nothing. We become aware that the question can only appear to be because the answer is present and insisting upon being revealed.

There is one question that seems to recur interminably. It is so persistent that it can seem to act as an obstacle to our complete spiritual perception. This question pertains to the appearance of evil. We have been told that evil is unreal. We have been told that it is a dream or an illusion. We can accept these answers because we have acknowledged the fact that God is All. Yet this one question continues to harass us: If God is All, why does evil *appear* to be real? If there really is no dreamer and no deluded mind, how can a dream or an illusion appear to be present in the experience of anyone?

It is not surprising that these questions should seem to be so persistent. In fact, it would be surprising if they did *not* continue to present themselves. You see, it would appear that every unanswered question indicates an absence of some aspect of the complete perception that God is All. Naturally, then, the question is going to continue to be in evidence until the complete answer is revealed. Once the Allness that is God is revealed fully and completely, it is impossible to be aware of further questions. This does not mean that all revelation has ceased. Quite the contrary—revelation is greater and more glorious than ever. But these revelations are simply an ever greater awareness of facts that have already been revealed.

We have had some answers to the question as to why evil should seem to be real, but for the most part, these answers have not been complete. The complete answer may be stated very simply and in very few words.

> There is no evil, and there is no one who is conscious of evil. There is not even a seeming evil condition or situation. Neither is there an identity who appears to be aware of an evil condition or situation.

Now, let us proceed to discover just what takes place and *why* it takes place when something *appears* to be evil.

Let us begin with our basic statement: God is All, All is God. The Allness that is God precludes the possibility of an evil presence, activity, or power. *This is why there is no evil.* This is basic Truth. But we must perceive something more if we are to experience the complete revelation of this fact. *Now we must realize what this appearance of evil is and why it appears to be seen, heard, known, or experienced.*

There is no universal imperfect fact. There is no omnipresent imperfection. Therefore, there can be no specific imperfect fact. There can be no presence that is an imperfect fact. Only that which is true—or a fact—can be evidenced. So there can be no evidence of imperfection. There can be no evidence of that which is not true, genuine, and perfect.

Any evidence of imperfection is imperfect evidence. It is faulty, misleading, and — if it is not perceived to be false — it can be deceptive. In short, it is a mistake to accept it or believe it. However, even the appearance of imperfect evidence serves a purpose, and this purpose is not evil. *If there is no evil, certain it is that no evil purpose can be served.*

Let us now perceive how it is, and why it is, that any *appearance* of evil is *not* evil — that it really serves a good purpose. If the fulfillment of any purpose is good, the impulsion behind this purpose has to be good and not evil. The mistake lies in our misconception of the meaning of that which we have called evil.

A mistake in mathematics is due to momentary ignorance of the perfect fact or principle of mathematics. An awareness of the perfect principle instantly corrects the mistake. The mistake has served to call your attention to the figure or figures that are right.

For instance, in solving a mathematical problem, it is possible to mistakenly write the figure 5 when the figure 4 should be written. This mistake will be evident throughout the entire procedure. Thus, the answer will be false, or untrue. Once the mistake is discovered, you are no longer concerned with it. Rather you are concerned only with that which is right and true, namely the figure 4. But the mistake has called your attention to the perfect mathematical principle. Thus the mistake has fulfilled a definite purpose.

Just as a mistake in mathematics calls your attention to the perfect mathematical fact, so it is that any appearance of evil serves to call your attention to some specific aspect of good, or God. God is Perfection; thus, Perfection is a universal as well as a specific fact. Any appearance of imperfection serves to call your attention to the perfect Principle, which is Perfection. *A mistake can seem to be troublesome or evil only so long as it is mistaken for a fact.* Once your attention is focused upon the perfect fact, the mistake is canceled. It simply vanishes.

Perfection is a universal fact. Imperfection is *not* a universal fact. Perfection is the specific fact. Imperfection is *not* the specific fact. Any appearance of imperfection but serves to focus your attention upon the Perfection which *does* exist. You know that only that which is a universal fact can be a specific fact.

You do not resist the mistake. You do not attempt to overcome it or to oppose it. You know it to be a mistake, and that ends it as far as you are concerned. The mistake has served its purpose, and your attention is now focused upon the perfect Principle. You keep your attention focused upon the universal and the specific fact until the evidence of this fact is apparent. You can never make a figure 5 become a figure 4. Neither can you make an appearance of imperfection become perfect. Your awareness of Perfection is the revelation and the evidence of that which is revealed.

Sickness, pain, disease, discord of any kind are not existent. They are not evidence of the perfect fact. Each is only an illusory appearance which serves to call your attention to the omnipresent fact which *does* exist. In this same way, apparent lack, trouble, or discord of any nature calls your attention to the universal Principle of supply, peace, joy, or harmony.

If you continue to be concerned with an appearance of discord, your attention remains focused upon a mistake. It is focused upon that which has already served its purpose and should be dismissed. So long as your attention continues to be focused upon a discordant appearance, that illusory appearance will continue to appear to be genuine. When you are constantly and consciously attentive to the perfect fact—*and only this fact*—the evidence of its presence is inevitable.

"Thou wilt keep him in perfect peace, whose mind is stayed on thee: because he trusteth in thee" (Isa. 26:3). To keep the attention constantly stayed on God is to hold firmly to the perfect Principle, or the existing fact. It is necessary to keep the attention focused upon the perfect fact if you are to have complete trust in God. *God is the perfect Fact.* God is the Entirety of your Existence, so the perfect Principle is your own Identity, your Life, your Consciousness, your Intelligence, and your Body. If you keep your Consciousness stayed on God, you are continuously aware of the Perfection which constitutes all there is of you. Perfection is omnipresent, so It remains present right where and when any appearance of discord calls your attention to its presence.

If apparent evil serves to draw your attention to God, or Good, then apparent evil is not evil, but good. It is God—who comprises your entire Existence—revealing Its Omnipresence. It makes no difference what the specific appearance of evil may be; the specific fact is already established in and as your own Consciousness. Your attention is simply being called to the specific fact. Thus, any appearance of evil must be but a signal signifying the presence of God, Good, Perfection. Now you perceive the truth of the statement, "There is no evil." You also realize why this statement is true.

The appearance of a material universe signifies the presence of the Universe of Light, or Spirit. The appearance of solidity signifies the presence of the Essence which is spiritual. An appearance of density, or darkness, signifies the presence of Light. The appearance of stupidity signifies the presence of Intelligence. In like manner, any appearance of temporal life, mind, consciousness signifies the presence of eternal Life, Intelligence, Consciousness.

The appearance of a personal "I"—assumptive man—signifies the presence of God evidencing Itself as the Identity. The assumptive "born body" signifies the eternal Body, comprised of Life, Mind, Consciousness. The assumption that there is a human mind centered in a brain signifies the presence of infinite

Intelligence, specifically identified. The appearance of a human consciousness, or life, is the signal announcing the presence of the infinite, eternal, conscious Life, identified as the specific conscious Life. That which is called human activity signifies the infinite Universe in action, or Omniaction, identified as specific activity. Our task is to keep the attention centered upon the universal, as well as the specific, Existence which is being signified.

Now let us perceive in what way this explanation of the signal, miscalled evil, may be helpful in our experience. We know that it is impossible to follow a method in this approach, so we will not consider the following to be a formula. Nevertheless, we can base our general contemplation upon the Truths that are here revealed, and we know that the right answers will be revealed within and as our own God-Consciousness. Certain it is that every statement you have read or are going to read here is absolute Truth.

We have said that any appearance of discord is but the signal for the infinite, eternal Perfection which is forever an established fact. We have realized that any fact that is a universal fact is a specific fact. We can now perceive the natural revelation and the evidence of the universal, yet specific, fact in the following way.

Suppose, for instance, you seem to be the victim of hatred or injustice. You know that any appearance of hatred would be the opposite of Love. You know that Love exists; thus, hatred does *not* exist. So the illusion called hatred is but the signal calling your attention to the presence of that which *does* exist, namely Love.

You do not dwell on the illusion, the signal, because it of itself is nothing. But you do not resist the signal. Neither do you oppose it. Rather you focus your attention entirely upon the universal—and specific—fact which *does* exist. And this fact is: God is Love. Yes, God is Love universally. God is Love specifically. You contemplate the innumerable and various ways in which this infinite Love is apparent as the perfect harmony of this Universe. You consider the wonderful way in which each star and planet fulfills its purpose in perfect harmony with the stars and planets which constitute this galaxy. You realize that this perfect, harmonious activity is Love in action. You also realize that Love is Intelligence; therefore, this universal activity is Intelligence acting lovingly. In this way, you have perceived the *impersonal* nature of Love. You have also realized that Love is a universal Truth, or fact.

Now, you may consider the perfect way in which our own Earth planet functions. The harmonious activity of this planet is perfect Love in action. *This same Love in action is all that is active in and as your experience.* This is being specific. This is realizing that universal, perfect Love is active in and as your specific existence. There is nothing to oppose this omnipotent, omniactive, perfect Love, and there is no one existing who can resist It. But this is not all;

there is no one who is genuinely conscious of anything that is contrary or opposite to this perfect, universal, infinite Love.

Your Consciousness is your Universe. This means that only that which comprises your Consciousness can be present, or evident, in or as your Life, your Consciousness, and your daily experience. Love alone is revealed as your Consciousness, so Love— and *only* Love—can be evidenced as your specific existence. This means that you are *not* aware of a supposititious opposite of Love, called hatred, in your daily affairs.

During this contemplation, you are intently alert. You do not permit an illusion of inactivity seemingly to put you to sleep. Neither do you aimlessly drift into an indifferent, indolent attitude. This is an active Truth.

During your contemplation of infinite Love will come a point at which a tremendous sense of peace and joy floods your entire Consciousness. But don't cease contemplating at this point. Joy is the harbinger of Love. Continue in your contemplation until you experience that great omnipotent surge of infinite Love. This is the apex of all your "seeing." Having reached this glorious height, you may now rest assured that you are truly seeing things as they are.

You may rest in this true perception, but you will not let your attention be distracted. You will not investigate to see whether or not the perfect fact, Love, is completely evidenced. You will not concern yourself with the signal—the seeming evil—again. You will "keep your mind stayed on God." You will discover that the Truth you have been perceiving is present; It is all that is, ever has been, or ever will be, present. But best of all, you will discover that the Truth you have perceived is *evident* right here and right now. Furthermore, the evidence will be all that *is* apparent, and it will be all that you are conscious of seeing or experiencing. Then it will appear that a healing has taken place. But you will know better. You will know that you have simply seen Existence as It is, and *the signal to draw your attention to this fact need never again appear.*

You have noted that we have gone quite thoroughly into the basic approach to the realization of Love, harmony, justice, perfection in your experience. There is nothing nebulous about this approach. It is most clear-cut and definite. Yet it must be revealed within and as your own Consciousness, and it will be *your own* revelation. However, it must be said that this same basic approach can be followed in every situation where inharmony of any kind appears.

It may be that an appearance of lack seems to be present. This is not evil. Rather it should be considered as merely the signal signifying the presence of infinite, omnipresent Supply. You will not approach this aspect of existence from the standpoint of the specific. Instead you will immediately contemplate the universal fact, which is omnipresent Supply.

This is a complete Universe. Its completeness precludes the possibility that anything could be missing that is necessary to Its Allness, Its Entirety. The realization of completeness is of vital importance in every situation where incompleteness, or lack, appears to be evident.

Actually, incompleteness, or lack, would seem to prevail in any illusion of trouble, disorder, or inharmony. It might appear as a lack of health, a lack of strength, a lack of joy or peace, or a lack of supply in the aspect called money. In any event, realization of the presence of that which *appears* to be absent is necessary if you are to experience the evidence of complete supply. Thus, it is apparent why the word *completeness* is of such vital importance.

Completeness is a universal fact. Thus, Supply is a universal fact. It is present everywhere, and It is present eternally. There are no vacuums in this universal fact, and there is no interruption of Its Presence. It is indivisible. It is that Principle which is omnipresent and inseparable from the specific Identity, which is God identified as you. It is within your Consciousness because It is constituted of your Consciousness. If you will realize that Supply, in any aspect, is as omnipresent as is Love, you will perceive the true nature of Supply. If you will "keep your mind stayed" on the presence of Supply — God — you will surely be aware of the evidence of this Presence right here and now.

Suppose a feeling of frustration or inadequacy seems to persistently present itself. It may appear that you are not fulfilling your purpose. It may seem that your activity is too limited or that your supply is limited by your present work or profession. Here again, it is essential to recognize the signal, then immediately to perceive the universal fact. This is an intelligent Universe. The Intelligence which comprises this perfect Universe is omniactive. Omniactive Intelligence acts intelligently, and thus It constantly fulfills Its purpose.

The universal purpose of omniactive Intelligence is the eternal, infinite maintenance and sustenance of absolute Perfection.

God, the Universe, is Self-maintained and Self-sustained. God, omniactive Intelligence, is ever active, maintaining Itself as eternal Perfection.

Your activity is inseparable from universal Omniaction. It can no more be an isolated activity than the activity of the wave can be isolated from the ceaseless movement of the ocean. The fulfillment of your purpose in being can never be divided from the purposeful fulfillment of the universal purpose. The fulfillment of purpose is universal, but it is also specific. The specific activity is essential to the completeness which is Omniaction. Therefore, your activity is absolutely necessary, and the fulfillment of your purpose in being is essential to the complete fulfillment of the universal completeness — the Totality which is God.

If it appears that you are not adequately fulfilling your purpose in being, this appearance can mean only that your attention has been called to this specific aspect of your completeness. The appearance of frustration signifies the presence of infinite fulfillment. It means that right here and now you are to perceive and to evidence the limitless fulfillment of your purpose in being. Consider these Truths. Consider them from the universal standpoint, then from the specific standpoint. If you will continue in this contemplation, you will find that your opportunities are limitless, and your profession, or work, is satisfying and fulfilling.

Sometimes it will seem that a decision must be made. It will appear that you do not know what course to pursue in some situation. This merely signifies that infinite Intelligence is present right here and now. It means that this omniactive Intelligence knows how to act and acts intelligently.

This is apparent when you consider the Perfection manifested as the omniactive Universe. There is no indecision, no wondering what to do, evident in the universal intelligent activity. The infinite Mind which acts knows how to act, when to act, and *acts*. The universal Mind in action is the Mind which is your Intelligence. The Intelligence that knows what Its activity should be, and *is*, is in full and complete operation as your own Intelligence right here and now. Had the answer not been already present, no question as to what course you should take would have arisen. In other words, the question is the signal that the answer is present within and as your Consciousness, insisting upon being revealed and evidenced.

Suppose that which is miscalled evil appears as symptoms of age, of change, of deterioration, or something that has to do with an aging mind or body. This appearance is exceedingly significant. It signifies the presence of beginningless, changeless, endless Existence. It signifies the universal fact that God, the Universe, is without beginning, change, or ending. It signifies the universal Consciousness of this fact. It signifies the fact that Life is eternal and imperishable and that the perfect Essence of all existence is indestructible. It is the signal for you to recognize the Eternality of your Life, Being, and Body. It means that eternity is now, and infinity is here. It means that the universal, imperishable Identity is being revealed as *your* Identity.

But this is not all. The signal has announced that *you* are the presence of the beginningless, changeless, endless Essence, and you are conscious of being this Essence. Therefore, you are aware of being the evidence of the universal fact which is revealing Itself as all there is of you. The Universe has not aged. The Universe has not deteriorated. Neither is It in the process of being destroyed. That which has been revealed as a universal Truth is true as your very Existence. You are this Truth, and you know it. Your knowing of this fact is the evidence of the Truth you know your Self to be.

Any unsatisfied longing signifies the presence of the satisfying and perfect fact. It may appear that you yearn for human satisfaction of some kind. But this seeming yearning is but the signal drawing your attention to the presence of the spiritual fact which satisfies. The presence of that which satisfies is your own divine Consciousness, aware of being eternally complete, lacking nothing that is essential to Its completeness.

A dinner bell is the signal announcing that the food is already prepared and you are free to partake of it. In this same way, any appearance of inharmony is but a signal announcing the presence of any perfect fact that is necessary to your complete harmony, perfection, and freedom. The dinner bell is not important of itself. It is not the food. Yet it signifies the presence of the food. You do not resist or resent the sound of the ringing of this bell. Rather you welcome it and act accordingly.

Suppose you misunderstood the sound of the bell. Suppose you misinterpreted it, and to you it signified danger or some horrendous event. In this case, you might appear to be fearful, angry, or resentful. Yet if you were to discover the true meaning of the signal, the fear, anger, or resentment would immediately disappear. Furthermore, the illusion of danger or anything of a catastrophic nature would have vanished. Above all, you would have discovered the genuine Presence—and the nature of the Presence—of that which the dinner bell signified. In other words, enlightened Consciousness reveals the Perfection which *is*, rather than the assumed imperfection which is *not*.

"But I say unto you, that ye resist not evil: but whosoever shall smite thee on thy right cheek, turn to him the other also" (Matt. 5:39). Jesus was well aware that evil was not what it appeared to be. He knew that resistance to that which appeared to be evil is failure to perceive the glorious Presence which is announcing Itself. He knew that evil of itself is nothing, but that the attitude toward it is exceedingly important.

You will remember his admonition pertaining to "the adversary." "Agree with thine adversary quickly, whiles thou art in the way with him; lest at any time the adversary deliver thee to the judge, and the judge deliver thee to the officer, and thou be cast into prison" (Matt. 5:25). Yes, indeed; it is well to agree with that which seems to be an adversary. And this agreement should be simultaneous with the first appearance of inharmony. If you resist or attempt to struggle with the so-called problem, you may seem to have to continue the struggle until you are bound tighter than ever, "cast into prison."

Jesus did not struggle when they came to arrest him in the Garden of Gethsemane. Neither did he attempt to defend himself against Pontius Pilate and his accusers. Jesus was, and is, a fully illumined Being, and he *knew,* and knows, the true nature of that which seemed to be evil. Furthermore, he knew *why* it apparently came into his experience.

Let us examine some other aspects in which the adversary may appear. Suppose, for instance, that you seem to suffer excruciating pain. This does seem to be your "trial by fire." Yet once you are free of this illusion, it is quickly forgotten. When the very first intimation of pain appears, it is well to realize instantly that *it is not evil.* It is not what it seems to be. Above all, do not resist it. Do not deny it and do not struggle with it.

"Agree with thine adversary." Acknowledge the signal; but know what it signifies. Consider the fact that evil is supposed to be the opposite of Good, or God. You *know* that All is God, Good, and there *is* no evil. So this seeming adversary is but a signal announcing the Presence of Good. If there were such a thing as evil, Good would be its opposite. So the appearance of pain signifies the presence of perfect harmony.

Here is the paradox. Pain certainly seems to be the opposite of Good. Yet it acts as a signal signifying the presence of the opposite of that which it appears to be. Thus, that which seems to be pain is not really evil. It is the exact opposite of the pain which it appears to be. I know this is most difficult to perceive. It is particularly difficult when one seems to be experiencing great suffering. But I also know that the realization of the foregoing facts, as stated, is evident as freedom from pain and imperfection. Here I speak from experience; thus, I can speak with solid conviction in sharing this revelation with you. Study and contemplation of the beginning statements in this paragraph will be most helpful and enlightening.

As you now perceive, apparent pain signifies the presence of perfect harmony. By this same token, that which seems to be weakness signifies the presence of strength. A mind that seems to be afraid signifies the presence of perfect Mind that has no awareness of fear. The Mind that is perfect Love knows nothing of fear. Rather It is unremittingly aware of perfect peace.

Suppose you seem to be suffering some so-called aftereffects of a former accident or illness. Right here is a tremendous Truth announcing Itself, ready to be fully revealed. This is the Truth which reveals the Body of Light. This Body is comprised of living, conscious, perfect Mind. This is the *only* Essence of the Body of Light, and there is no other body.

The eternal Body of Light is immutable. It does not change, and nothing has happened — or *can* happen — to change It. It was never invaded by an illness of any nature. Never did It experience an accident. Its Essence is immutable, eternal Light, Spirit, and It could not be injured or in any way depleted. Being eternal by Its very nature, It is incapable of beginning or ending. It can never suffer; It can never perish or be destroyed.

In the perfect, orderly, harmonious Universe of Light, no accident could ever happen. Thus, the Body of Light could never suffer as a result of something that never took place. It is not subject to the spurious laws of man. It is free from the cruel but fallacious laws called laws of nature. Its only Nature is the Nature of infinite, eternal, immutable Existence. Never was It born. It is completely free from any illusions pertaining to heredity or to nonexistent prenatal causes. It is conscious, living Light. It is constantly aware of the Perfection which It is. Its awareness of being Perfection is without a vacuum and without an interruption.

That which is called evil may appear as abnormal activity of the body. It could appear as retarded or accelerated activity. It could appear as obstructed activity, or it could appear as activity that had ceased entirely. Anything that has to do with activity signifies the presence of Omniaction. Right here and right now, the universal, rhythmic, omnipotent Omniaction, which is God in action, is announcing Itself. Can the drop of water act contrary to the wave? Can the wave go against the tide? Can the tide go against the ocean? Can the Earth planet retard or accelerate the rhythm of its activity? Can the stars and planets change the rhythm of their orbiting? No! No! No! Neither can the body or any aspect of the body act or react in any way that is opposed to the omniactive Omnipotence which is God in action.

Perhaps it may appear that something has been added to the body. This illusion signifies its opposite, the presence of immutable Completeness. The changeless, birthless, deathless Body of Light is here and now being revealed. The body is complete *as itself*. Every aspect of the body is complete. There is nothing existing in or as the body that is not essential to its completeness. There is nothing included in or as the body that is not essential to the perfect fulfillment of its purpose. There is nothing present as the body that is not necessary to its eternal harmony and perfection.

Nothing can be added to or subtracted from the eternally perfect Body of Light—and there are *not* two bodies. There is one alone, and this one Body of Light is as complete and as immutable as is the Universe of Light. It is not subject to invasion. In fact, there is nothing of an inharmonious nature to invade It. Its Essence is conscious, living, loving Mind, and this is the Essence that comprises the Universe. An abnormal growth is unknown. There is no awareness of a blemish or a flaw. There is no mind that can know an abnormality of any kind.

God knows what God is. Even God could not know what God is not. Thus, the Mind that is God knows Itself to be immutably perfect. The Body of Light is Self-conscious. It knows what It is. It can know nothing other than that which It is, and It can know nothing that is unknown to God, the only Mind that knows anything.

Oh, there is power in this realization! I know of no Truth that is more powerful than is the Truth that God knows *only* Its eternal, immutable Perfection. Consider this Truth. Welcome the signal that brings your attention to this dynamic Truth. In other words, "agree with thine adversary."

It may seem that the vision is impaired or the hearing inadequate. Right here the all-seeing Eye or the all-hearing Ear is revealing Itself. The Vision that is God is not dimmed; neither is the all-hearing Ear impaired. Vision is Consciousness infinitely perceiving Its own perfection. Hearing is this same Consciousness hearing the beauty of Its own perfection. The eyes are not vehicles through which the infinite Vision is strained. Rather they are the very Vision Itself. The ears are not vessels through which the infinite Ear hears. Rather they are comprised of the Essence which is the all-hearing Ear.

Never attempt to divide Vision into personal visions. Never consider hearing to be separated into little personal blocks of hearing. Vision and Hearing are the one infinite Consciousness actively aware of Itself. There is One who sees and One who hears. And because there is no other, your seeing, your hearing is this One seeing and hearing Itself. It is not "I" that sees, but God who sees as my Vision. It is not "I" that hears, but God who hears as my Hearing. That which I see, I am. That which I hear, I am. I can never be separate from or other than my Self. Therefore I can never be separate from or other than my complete, conscious, perfect Vision and my perfect Hearing. That which I am, I see. That which I am, I hear, for I am *that* I AM. The Vision infinite is the only Vision I know. The Hearing infinite is the only Hearing I am.

Can the signal which has drawn my attention to this universal fact be evil? Indeed no. The signal is the Consciousness I am, saying, "I am the Vision that faileth not. I am the Hearing that can never be depleted." I welcome the signal because I welcome God's revelation of Itself as my seeing and my hearing.

Perhaps it may appear that some aspect of the body is infected. Is the Body of the Universe infected? Does God infect Itself? The Essence of the Body of Light is not separate from the Essence which comprises the Body of the Universe. The universal Essence does not stop at the outline of the Body of Light. The Consciousness which is Spirit knows nothing of infection. The false appearance has but focused my attention upon the immutable, eternal Spirit which constitutes the entirety of my Body of Light. This is also your Body of Light.

If the body could be infected, God would have to be infected. But this is not all—God would have to *know* Itself to be both the infection and the infected body. This is, of course, ridiculous, but it would have to be the situation if infection were genuine. After all, God *is* All. All *is* God.

It may appear that some aspect of the body is deteriorating or that it has decayed. Perhaps it could be called tuberculosis or tooth decay. Right here and right now, the pure, changeless Wholeness which is God is announcing Itself. "And what agreement hath the temple of God with idols? for ye are the temple of the living God; as God hath said, I will dwell in them, and walk in them; and I will be their God, and they shall be my people" (I Cor. 6:16).

The temple of God is not desecrated. Jesus knew that the temple of the living God was his Body. He even referred to his Body as being the indestructible temple. "Destroy this temple, and in three days I will raise it up" (John 2:19). The Essence which comprises the temple—Body of Light—is imperishable. It cannot be destroyed. Neither does It destroy Itself. Living Intelligence is not Self-destructive. It would not be intelligent for Life to destroy Itself. Neither would it be Love in action.

The Body of Light eternally remains holy (wholly) perfect and immutable. The Wholeness and the inviolate Allness which is God comprises the Wholeness and the Entirety of the Body of Light. There is no body of darkness overshadowing the Body of Light. Neither is there a shadow of density that can conceal this glorious, whole, complete, immutable Body of Light. It can no more decay or deteriorate than can the Universe Itself. There can be no knowledge of destruction or impairment. There is no mind to know such phantasmic illusions. That which is unknown to God *remains* unknown. *There is no intelligence other than God to know anything.*

The signal has focused your attention upon the indestructible, imperishable nature of the Body of Light. It has meant the opening of your eyes, that you might see, perceive, the immutable Wholeness which is God revealing Itself as the *only* Essence of the form. It has signified the glory that is God revealing Itself to be the glorious Body of Light.

Sometimes it may seem that the body is arthritic. This would seem to be a condition that is painful and that interferes with the freedom of the body. Here again, the attention has been drawn to the perfect freedom of universal Consciousness. Living, conscious Intelligence is never hampered. Its activity is never curtailed. Most important of all is the fact that the unconditioned infinite Mind knows nothing of conditions. Neither does It know aught of degrees of perfection and imperfection. It knows only Itself.

There are no conditions in this Universe. God, the Universe, is unqualified, unconditioned Perfection. Any difficulty that seems to be apparent in or as the body would have to be considered a condition. But the forever-established Perfection which constitutes the Body of Light is Its own immunity to any and all illusory conditions. A condition would imply change. God, the Universe, is eternally immutable. There can be no change and no condition which implies change in the everlasting, living, conscious Mind which is God. That is why there can be no change and no condition in or as *your* Body of Light. The universal, unconditioned Consciousness can have no awareness of change. It can be conscious only of Its unconditioned, immutable Self. This is *your* Consciousness. This is the Essence that constitutes your Body of Light.

"The light of the body is the eye: if therefore thine eye be single, thy whole body shall be full of light" (Matt. 6:22). Yes, the Body of Light *is* apparent when the enlightened Consciousness is aware of *only* the Body of Light.

Once this perfect Body is seen, known, and experienced, you can never be deceived or deluded as to its Essence. You *know,* beyond any doubt, that the perfect, eternal, immutable Body of Light is the only Body. Furthermore, you know that your Body of Light consists of the Consciousness you *are,* fully aware of being the eternal, changeless Perfection which you know your Self to be. And so it is, and thus it remains.

Chapter XI

The Ultimate Answer

And he shall judge among many people, and rebuke strong nations afar off; and they shall beat their swords into plowshares, and their spears into pruning-hooks: nation shall not lift up a sword against nation, neither shall they learn war any more ... For all people will walk every one in the name of his god, and we will walk in the name of the Lord our God for ever and ever.

— Mic. 4:3,5

In these verses from Micah we perceive the ultimate answer to the seemingly hopeless problems of the world today. These verses are often quoted and written as a sign of hope for a fear-ridden world. However, the hope is for a *future* world of peace. Thus these quotations are considered to be prophetic. But are they a prophecy? Indeed they are not. And a careful study and contemplation will reveal the fallacy of this misconception.

Micah was experiencing illumination when he made these wonderful statements. He was not prophesying something that would come to pass in some distant future. Rather he was actually seeing things *as they were and are.* His eyes were opened, and he perceived the Actuality which appears to be hidden from the mind and vision of assumptive man.

It is not surprising that these words of Micah should be considered prophetic. What is seen in illumination is diametrically opposite to the world as it *appears* to be. That explains why so many wonderful statements in the Bible are interpreted as prophecies. No doubt the *appearance* of a troubled world was just as apparent to the peoples of biblical days as it is to us today.

As we have stated, throughout the ages there have been those who experienced illumination. They too saw the world of peace and perfection, even as did Micah. Yet the world has gone right on pursuing its own illusions, and there has been no genuine enlightenment among the general public as to *how* this phantasmic situation can be obliterated. But Micah gives us the answer to this. It is found in the last sentence of the quotation: "… and we will walk in *the name of the Lord our God* for ever and ever."

Indeed we *will* walk in the name of the one and only Identity. We *know* the name of our God. It is I AM. We will walk, live, move, and have our being as the one I AM Identity. This is the answer to the entire *appearance* of a world filled with trouble, wars, and the rumors of wars. This must and *will* be the realization and the experience of each and every one of us because enlightened Consciousness is the *only* Consciousness, right here and right now.

To walk in the name of the Lord our God means to walk as illumined Beings. This does not mean to experience only an occasional flash of illumination.

These occasional experiences of enlightened Consciousness are wonderful, but something more is required if we are to realize constant peace and perfection. This something more is the steady, uninterrupted experience of illumination.

Our first conscious experiences of illumination are usually brief. More often than not, they last but a moment or two. Sometimes they may seem to appear and disappear so quickly that we wonder whether or not the experience is genuine. Then, too, a period of great illumination may be followed by that which seems to be a great depression, frustration, or even inharmony. It is as if one had been in a brilliantly lighted room and had suddenly stepped out into a very dark night. The light was so bright that the darkness seems darker than ever. Of course, this latter experience is not genuine. It is just that in illumination the ecstasy has been so tremendous that *any* seeming descent from this ecstasy seems very dark indeed.

There is one certainty in any experience of illumination. Having seen Actuality as It is, you can never again be satisfied with the world of appearance. For this reason, you will keep right on and eagerly await the next illumination. This is good, because all the while, you are experiencing longer periods of enlightenment, and you *are* approaching the steady, constant, uninterrupted realization of the Universal Light which constitutes your Being and the Being of All. Aware of seeing and being this Universal Light, you are aware of uninterrupted Perfection. It makes no difference how real the illusion of imperfection may *appear* to be; you are not deceived. You know, and *you know that you know*. You live perfectly normal lives. You do nothing that is irrational or foolish. It is just that you go quietly on your way, seeing what you see and being what you see, despite all appearances of discord or inharmony.

Living as an illumined Being is very much like walking around in the midst of a dream world yet being wide awake. This does not mean that you are blind to the seeming troubles of others. Always you are understanding and compassionate. *Love is ever compassionate.* It is true that you recognize the *appearance* of trouble and of seemingly troubled ones. You know how real it seems to them. You know the seeming nature of the trouble, whether it appears to be illness, lack, or whatever, but you also know that it actually *is not an experience.* Furthermore, you know that the seemingly troubled one is untouched by the dream or illusion. This is what it means to walk in the full realization of our eternal, immutable, infinite Identity, I AM.

It is paradoxical that this great wealth of Light should abide right here, where an impoverished world of darkness appears to be so real. Yet that is the way it appears, and we do not ignore this appearance. To do so would be unloving and without compassion. Being Love, we *act* lovingly. This being true, let us calmly and intelligently consider this world of appearance. Let us discover *what* it is and why all the efforts to bring peace and harmony into it have apparently failed. Many and valiant have been, and are, the efforts to bring peace to the world. This is true because inherently we *know* that peace and harmony are normal, while war, unrest, and inharmony are abnormal.

We have no quarrel with those who are trying to improve world conditions. On the contrary, we commend them, knowing the sincerity and the unselfish motives inherent in most of their efforts. Yet we cannot ignore or be blind to the fact that all efforts to improve the world of appearance have failed to produce any permanent improvement. On the contrary, the situation as it stands today seems to be more troubled and more dangerous than ever before. This despite the honest, sincere work of the United Nations, of the religious organizations of the world, and of certain unselfish individuals. If *any* organization or individual could have brought peace to the world of appearance, the League of Nations would have accomplished this years ago. But such was not the case.

Now let us see *why* it has proved impossible to bring peace to the world. No assumptive human being and no group or organization of human beings *can* solve the problems of a world of their own making. You see, this seemingly troubled world is comprised of the very same illusory "mind of man" that is attempting to solve its problems. No problem can be solved from the level of the problem. "Let them alone: they be leaders of the blind. And if the blind lead the blind, both shall fall into the ditch" (Matt. 15:14).

What Jesus was really saying here is that no dreamer can awaken another dreamer from his dreams. No deluded one can arouse another from his illusion. Jesus was well aware of the fact that the dream and the dreamer are the same one, and this one is completely devoid of Life, Consciousness, Mind, Actuality. He used words, as all of us do, to try to explain what did not exist.

Negotiations are futile because they are based upon a false premise — the premise of "getting." Each negotiator approaches the negotiating table with the hope of obtaining advantage *over* the one, or ones, with whom he is negotiating. Even the churches cannot bring peace and harmony to the negotiating table, because they are not at peace with one another.

Any human government must be faulty. This is true whether it pertains to the government of a city, state, nation, or whether it pertains to the government of the world. The attempt to dominate and enslave the entire world is but the fallacious little "I," swollen to its greatest misconception of itself.

Centuries ago Lao-tzu, the greatly illumined Chinese philosopher, stated, "A leader is best when people barely know that he exists." This is a tremendous Truth, and it has its basis in the fact that the less of the little "I" there is in evidence, the more the genuine and only *I* is being realized and manifested. The little "I" is incapable of governing intelligently because it is not the one and only genuine Intelligence which is God. God makes no mistakes.

The root of all difficulty between nations, states, or cities is *dualism*. It is dualism that draws imaginary lines, calling them boundaries *between* nations and peoples. It is dualism which separates religion into religions and sets churches and their leaders against one another. It is dualism that makes one assumptive man consider himself to be a leader. This, of course, means that those who look up to a leader must of necessity consider themselves to be followers. Thus, they limit themselves, even to the point of considering themselves to be inferior to or beneath the so-called leader.

It is small wonder that primitive, savage cruelty has seemed to be practiced and still seems to be in evidence today. You see, dualism enters into the earliest records of primitive man. In the illusion of materiality, he is recorded to have feared anything which he considered to be outside of, or other than, himself. Thus, he feared the sun, the moon, the rain, the night, and the wind. His first reaction was to propitiate these unknown powers, so he made images of them and imagined them to be gods. Later, he is recorded to have become more enlightened and to have offered sacrifices to but one God. Still, this one God was a power and a presence that was separate from himself.

As they apparently feared God, it is not surprising that assumptive men should fear and distrust each other. Neither is it surprising that boundary lines should be established, and these assumed boundaries were to separate tribes, nations, and continents. It is in this same way that those of religious convictions apparently inaugurated separate churches, separate faiths, and separate practices in their worship of a God outside—or other than—their own infinite Selfhood.

Of course, the foregoing is only an illusory concept of Existence, and it is futile to pursue it any further. It is sufficient to explain the fallacy of dualism and to perceive that it is the basis of our seemingly troubled world today.

Before we can continue, there is another most important fact that must be perceived. If the perception of this fact is not perfectly clear, the realization of omnipresent freedom, perfection, and peace will not be complete. Let us pinpoint that which seems to be the greatest fear of assumptive man. This illusory fear is based on the false premise that the body is temporal and that it can be destroyed. It is also assumed that the destruction of this born body means death, or an end to the life which is supposed to be born *into* this body.

It is true that most religions assure their followers that the soul survives the death of the body. Thus, most members of any religious group have at least a hope of survival. But somehow life seems to be inexorably associated with the born body of "man with breath in his nostrils." So the illusory fear is that the body will be destroyed, thus depriving the identity of the only kind of life he seems to understand. Of course, this hallucination includes the fear that *all* life will be destroyed.

If the genuine nature of the eternal, imperishable, indestructible Body were known, there would be no illusion of fear that It could be destroyed. If the Essence of all Life were known to be Spirit, or Consciousness, it would also be known that any attempt to destroy Life would be futile. Thus the fear or dread of a threat to Life would be obliterated, and the power-mad assumptive little men would see the futility of war.

In other words, when it is known that Life, Consciousness, Intelligence, Love constitute the entire Essence and activity of the Universe and the body, there will be no more incentive for war.

Now, we have presented much — too much — about what only *seems* to exist. Let us now consider the genuine and *only* Existence which does exist.

We have stated over and over that God is All, All is God. We have also said that God is the Universe, and this means that the Universe consists of God. We know that God is indivisible and cannot be separated into sections of Itself. Thus, this is an indivisible Universe, and this indivisible Universe is completely free of boundaries. The infinite Life that lives continues to be the same inseparable Life whether It is evidenced in China, in England, in Russia, Germany, or in the United States of America. The indivisible Consciousness remains identically the same Consciousness regardless of where It is evidenced. The inseparable, intelligent Love which is God remains the same loving Intelligence no matter where It is in evidence. Wherever there is intelligent Love, there is conscious Life. *And where is there not conscious, living, intelligent Love? Where is there no God?* The inseparability of universal, conscious, intelligent, living Love is evidenced as the inseparability of nations and of peoples.

Right now it would be well to remind ourselves of one salient fact: there is no such thing as space or time. Even though we have referred to other nations and peoples, let us not be deceived. There can be no "other" nations and peoples because there is but one indivisible, omnipresent Consciousness. There is no other consciousness to be conscious. Furthermore, the Consciousness *you* have — and are — is equally present and simultaneously present, universally; thus, there can be no "there" to you. There is no time involved in the focusing of your attention anywhere; thus, there can be no time to you.

Right now your attention is focused upon the words you are reading. Yet your Consciousness does not end abruptly at the page. In fact, It does not end at all. The page does not act as a line of demarcation that separates your Consciousness. Furthermore, you are just as conscious right where the page is as you are conscious right where the eyes are. You are equally as conscious throughout the entire room, and the walls do not enclose or partition the Consciousness you are. Thus, you can actually recognize no genuine space separating you from the page you are reading or from the entire room.

In this same way, you can realize that there are no lines of demarcation that separate you from any nation in the world. Your Consciousness is conscious simultaneously where your attention is focused on the page and throughout the room. It is also present simultaneously throughout the world and the timeless, spaceless Universe.

Never imagine that you can confine the Consciousness you have and are. Even though it may appear that you draw imaginary lines of demarcation around your Consciousness, it is impossible to confine the unconfinable. It appears that your Consciousness is confined only so long as you imagine this to be true.

Let us consider a simple example of this fact. Once during a sojourn in a small town in Nevada, I noted the cowboys and their horses. When they dismounted prior to entering a store, they never tied or hitched their horses to a post or a rail of any kind. Rather they just dropped the reins to the ground and walked away. The horse would stand quietly for the most part, and even when it moved, it would move only in a very small circular area. After having observed this phenomenon on several occasions, I asked a cowboy, "How does it happen that your horse does not run away? It is not tied to anything, and it is free. What holds it right at this point?"

The cowboy smiled and replied, "No, ma'am; he isn't tied. He certainly *could* walk or run away at any moment. But he has been trained this way. You see, he *thinks* he is tied right here and that he can move only in this small circle."

Well, it would *seem* that we too have been trained. It would seem that our entire training was based upon the fallacy of limitation. The illusory misconception of dualistic division and separation has seemed to act as lines of demarcation to us. These imaginary lines of demarcation have apparently deceived us. They have made us imagine that our activity is confined to a small enclosed circle. Thus, we have not been cognizant of our undivided, omniactive Consciousness, which is universal, omnipresent, and eternal.

Of course, this is understandable when we consider the seeming world of appearance. Everything that appears to be material substance seems to be separate from its surroundings. It would appear that Life existing as a living tree is confined within the outline of the tree. It would also appear that Life existing as a living body is confined within the outline of the body. The living body is a conscious, intelligent body, so the illusion would have us believe that living, conscious Intelligence is blocked off — encircled and separated — by the outline of the body.

However, we *know* that the conscious, living, loving Mind which constitutes the Essence of the body is unconfined. We know that the outline, or the delineation of the form, does not separate Life into lives, Consciousness into consciousnesses, Mind into minds, or Love into loves. There is a definite purpose in this reminder at this point. The purpose will become apparent as you continue to read and to contemplate the truths you are reading.

"Ye are the light of the world. A city that is set on a hill cannot be hid" (Matt. 5:14). The enlightened Consciousness you are is the Light of the world. It is inevitable that this illumined Consciousness be recognized and accepted universally. It has to be thus, you see, for God—this Consciousness—cannot be hidden. The enlightened Consciousness you have, and *are*, is universal and indivisible, and you are aware of this fact. *It is in your awareness of this fact that the Light which you are is "the light of the world."* If the enlightened Consciousness you are could be divided and confined within a given area, you could *not* be the Light of the world. But you know that the Consciousness you are is unconfined, because It is not blocked off in blocks of nonexistent time or space.

Beloved, it is you knowing your indivisible, universal Nature that makes you the Light of the world.

Never limit the power of your enlightened Consciousness. Recognize the fact that the universal, impersonal Love you *are* is omnipotent, omnipresent Love. Accept the glorious fact that the Love you are is power and that It is the *only* power in existence. Don't try to personalize It. Don't limit It by circumscribing It between imaginary limited boundaries. *Let* It flow and surge as unlimited joy and peace.

There is the entire power of universal Love in your realization of being universal and indivisible. The Truth you know is true everywhere. Your Consciousness, aware of this Truth, is equally present everywhere. Therefore, there is an awareness of this Truth everywhere.

You cannot contemplate selfishly. You cannot really draw a line of demarcation around your contemplation, hugging it to yourself. Your Consciousness, in contemplation, is too big for that. As you know, It is infinite.

By this same token, you cannot *use* the Truth you perceive in silent contemplation. Least of all can you use It selfishly. *Your only power lies in the fact that you are every truth you know to be true.* If you were to attempt to *use* the universal Intelligence that you are, the Mind you are would be incomplete. It would not be loving to limit the power of this Truth—if this were possible—through a selfish attempt to use It for your own little personal purposes. But the infinite, conscious Love you are will know better than to make any such attempt.

No, you do not attempt to confine your contemplation to your own affairs. By this same token, you do not attempt to confine your contemplation to the affairs of your immediate vicinity—your city, your state, or your nation. Rather you recognize the universal, indivisible nature of every Truth you are perceiving, and you know that this Truth is equally present and equally active as the Consciousness of each and every Identity in the city, the state, the nation, and the world. You are fully cognizant of the fact that this is not the way the world *appears* to be. Yet you remain steadfast in your realization that *this is the way it is.*

Now, you may wonder just how this universal approach can be helpful to a world in such great turmoil and strife. You may question its practicality or its efficacy. In fact, you may ask, "Does it work? Is it provable?" Indeed, it *does* work. It *is* provable. But *you* do not prove it. Rather it proves itself just by reason of its being true.

Any truth can be proven. It can be proven because it is true. Any untruth cannot be proven because it is not true. Oh, it can temporarily be made to *appear* to be true, but an *appearance of an untruth cannot prove that which is true.* The proof of any truth lies in the evidence of its existence. There is such abundant evidence of the truth of this approach that an entire book could not state all of the testimony that has been offered as proof of its practicality. If this were just a beautiful theory, it should be written as a myth or a fairy tale. If this Truth were merely an impractical theory, this book would not have been written.

Now let us perceive just how this Truth proves Itself to be true. Let us perceive why Its truth is evidenced in and as the affairs of the world, the nation, states, cities, and the affairs of the specific Identity. The following reports will reveal the how and the why of this practical approach.

The textbook on this particular approach is entitled *The Ultimate,* and it was published in 1957. Here in California, we have conducted four seminars. There are students of *The Ultimate* in almost every country in the world, and of course, throughout the United States. Notices of the seminars were mailed to those students on our mailing lists. Of course, it was not possible for many of them to attend the seminars, and we *knew* that those who could not attend could also be inspired and enlightened during our sessions. So we invited them to "tune in" during the hours when we were in session. Many of them did tune in, and their experiences were glorious proofs of the universal inseparableness of Consciousness and of the Truth we were perceiving.

Almost immediately following each seminar, letters arrived from students of *The Ultimate* in this country and in other countries of the world. They had checked the hours of the sessions and had tuned in during those hours. Some of these sincere students remained awake most of the night, and others did not sleep at all during the nights of the seminars. Their experiences were tremendously inspiring and rewarding. For instance, many students who had never before consciously experienced illumination suddenly discovered that they *were* illumined. But this is not all.

Many of the very revelations *we* were experiencing were being experienced by those who were tuned in. An interesting point is that the sequence of their revelations was exactly the order in which we experienced them. One student wrote what was revealed *as it was being revealed.* Our records show that the words and sentences she was hearing were identically the same words and sentences that were being spoken at the seminar. Furthermore, each word and each sentence was in its right context and in its right sequence. Herein is proof that the enlightened Consciousness *is* indivisible and that there is neither time nor space.

It is exceedingly important that you realize *how* these wonderful experiences took place and *why* the students were able to have them. But first it is necessary for you to know what did *not* take place and why it *could not* have taken place.

This was not mental telepathy. We did not project thoughts. We did not mentally reach out to anyone. Those who tuned in did not reach out to us. We did not concentrate. We did not meditate. In fact, what we did was the exact opposite of mental telepathy, of concentration, of meditation.

Knowing that Consciousness is infinite and indivisible, we knew that we could not send out thoughts. *Knowing that this same Consciousness is equally present everywhere,* we could not project revelations. We knew that concentrated meditation is an activity of the assumptive mind and that this assumptive mind is illusory and necessarily limited. So in full, open Consciousness we contemplated. *To contemplate is to calmly, consciously consider Existence as It is. That is what we did, and that is all that we did.*

Now let us perceive how it was, and why it was, that our contemplation—and our revelations during contemplation—were revealed throughout the world and throughout our own country. *It was all a matter of Consciousness. It was a matter of our awareness of being boundless, indivisible, universal, omnipresent Consciousness.*

The term *tune in* may give a false impression of what took place. Actually, it was not a matter of "tuning in" at all, but we have used that expression for want of a better way of explaining this experience.

In order to explain the foregoing glorious experiences further, we will now record what was realized prior to the seminars and during the hours of the sessions. Those students who could not attend were told that it was possible for them to experience the revelations we were experiencing, and in the following way: each student should reflect upon the infinite, universal nature of Consciousness, Mind, Intelligence. He should consider the boundless heavens and the fact that this Universe was, and is, the Omnipresence called God, or Consciousness. He could contemplate the inseparable nature of conscious Intelligence. He could consider the fact that this boundless, indivisible Consciousness is conscious as *his* Consciousness and that therefore his Consciousness is not limited to or bound by oceans, continents, or countries.

He could reflect upon the timeless, spaceless, boundless Consciousness which comprises this Universe and realize that this is his own Consciousness. In this way he could realize that he was unconfined and that we also were unconfined. He could realize that the Consciousness we were, contemplating Existence, was exactly the same Consciousness *he* was, in the same contemplation. He could know that because Consciousness is indivisible, the Consciousness we were—and are—was where he was, and the Consciousness he is was where we were. How, then, could he fail to be aware of the revelations which we were experiencing? He could not, and the fact that he did not fail is evidenced in the many letters we received reporting his revelations.

Instead of concentrating and meditating, our Consciousness was completely open and free. Instead of sending or projecting thoughts, we were aware of the inseparability of the Truths we were perceiving. Instead of mental effort, we experienced completely effortless revelations. In this way, there were no mental manipulations and no mental gymnastics. And this is the way it must ever be in our particular approach.

I have explained as thoroughly as possible just how it was possible for us to have exactly the same revelations simultaneously, although to all appearances we were supposedly separated by states, continents, and oceans. Why this was possible is easily explained. It was possible because we *knew* the genuine nature of our being. We knew that we were inseparable and that there could be no lines of demarcation where one of us left off, or ended, and another of us began. We knew that Truth is a universal Existent and that every Truth is equally present everywhere. Furthermore, we knew that the enlightened Consciousness, which is aware of all Truth, is the only Consciousness that *could* be conscious as each one of us. All of this we knew without effort or meditation. We simply knew it as full, open, infinite Consciousness.

There is definite purpose in this presentation of our experiences during the seminars. This purpose is to enable every one of us to contemplate lovingly and intelligently upon the affairs of the world today. The very same procedure that has just been presented, pertaining to the seminars, can be followed when contemplating the world and its activities.

It has been said that no nation is higher than the intelligence of its people. I can assure you that *the enlightened Consciousness of the people is the only means of freedom, peace, and perfect government*. That which is true of a nation is also true of the world. That which is true of the world is true of each Identity. Above all, it is a universal Truth; thus Its truth must be universally perceived and evidenced.

Those of us who are consciously illumined, or enlightened, really are "the light of the world." The Consciousness we are — and we know ourselves to be — cannot be hidden. The "city that is set on a hill" is our enlightened Consciousness. The Light we are *must* be the Light of the world. Enlightened Consciousness dispels all seeming darkness and ignorance. Intelligent Love cancels all selfishness and hate. Principle obliterates all assumptive, unprincipled forces, and the perception that God is indivisibly All dispels all illusions of separateness, of division. Indeed, we *are* the Light of the world, *but we must be conscious of this fact, and we must be actively engaged in our contemplation of this fact, if we are to fulfill our purpose in being this Light.*

So let us continue our exploration of just how to fulfill this tremendously important purpose.

From our wonderful experiences during the seminars, it is apparent that our revelations were not confined to what would be called our immediate vicinity, to the state of California, or to the United States. In this same way, you can realize that your awareness of Truth is not confined to your state or to your country. You can be sure that the Truth you are perceiving is being revealed throughout the entire world.

Furthermore, you can be assured that the Consciousness you are, being actively conscious of this Truth, is the Consciousness of every Identity in existence being aware of this Truth. *Oh, there is power in this realization.* There is the power of infinite Love. And the power is as limitless as is the Love that engenders it.

Now, it may occur to you that those who tuned in during the seminars were actively seeking the Light and that they were deliberately maintaining a full open Consciousness. *Never limit anyone.* No matter how far from the Light the Consciousness may appear to be, remind yourself that the *only* Consciousness being conscious *is* enlightened. Furthermore, you have no way to know how many Identities there are, throughout the world, who are seeking the Light. Everyone whose Consciousness is open will be aware of the Truth that you are *actively* perceiving. And you do not know how many there are who are already actively, consciously enlightened, or illumined.

It is a well-known fact that what is called distance is no barrier in Consciousness. Often a practitioner will receive a call for help from someone who is supposedly thousands of miles distant, perhaps on the other side of the world. Furthermore, the one who calls for help almost always receives and acknowledges this help. This is called absent treatment, but because Consciousness is indivisible, there really is no absent treatment. The Consciousness of the one called practitioner and the one called patient remains the same inseparable Consciousness. Therefore, there can be no line of demarcation that would act as a dividing line between them.

It is true that there really is but one Consciousness, and no illusory sense of existence can change this fact. Neither can an illusion called "man with breath in his nostrils" usurp the existence of this one enlightened Consciousness. This may, perhaps, be your first realization in contemplating the world: first, the indivisible Omnipresence of enlightened Consciousness, then the fact that this enlightened Consciousness is the only Consciousness.

In our contemplation, we will never descend to the level of that which appears to be the problem. There are many sincere Christians who are earnestly praying for peace. They have faith in God as they understand God, and sometimes this great faith of itself does wonders. We do not discount the efficacy of their prayers. Then, too, there are many metaphysicians who are daily doing "mental work" for the world. They too are sincere, and we know that ofttimes wonderful things take place through the mental work of those who practice metaphysics.

We place no limitations upon the prayers of the Christians or upon the mental work of the metaphysicians. When we refer to Christians or metaphysicians, we are referring to those of *all* religious faiths—those of the Orient, those of Asia, as well as those of our Western World. We recognize the fact that every prayer is a prayer for the good of the world. We are also cognizant that all metaphysical work is based on the Omnipotence which is God, and we consider all of this to be good. We welcome it, and we are happy that it is going on. However, they pray or "work" from the standpoint that there *is* a problem to be solved. And this is not our way.

The entire basis of our contemplation is the Allness, the Onliness, which is God, Good, Perfection, and we pay no attention to the illusory problem. To us there cannot be God and a problem which is not God.

We contemplate from the standpoint of the perfect, harmonious Universe which is God. We consider the infinite Intelligence which is evidenced as the orderly activity of the galaxies, the stars, and the planets. We perceive the harmony and the peace which is manifested as the perfect Universe. We know that this peace and this harmony indicate the presence of Love. Our Consciousness is "full open." We consider the fact that our galaxy is but one of innumerable galaxies, that our sun is but one of countless suns, and our Earth planet is but one little pinpoint in the illimitable, immeasurable, boundless Universe. Thus, our perspective is universal.

Furthermore, the universality of our perspective of Existence includes the eternality of It and the eternality of all that is necessary to Its completeness. Thus, we are aware of the eternality of every galaxy, every star and planet, and our Earth planet. That which is eternal is, by its very nature, immutable. So the word *immutability* may now be important in our contemplation. It is noteworthy right here that any word that is necessary at the moment will appear in and as our Consciousness.

Now, we have been, and are, aware of many universal Truths. For instance, we are aware that this Universe consists of indivisible Consciousness. We have also perceived that It consists of Intelligence and Love. We have realized that It is complete, eternal, and immutable. We have perceived that these are not qualities or attributes *of* this Universe but that *they constitute this boundless Immensity.* Thus, they are inseparable.

You will note that we have not taken the illusion called matter into consideration at all. We have not considered the stars and the planets to be bodies of matter. There is nothing material about Mind, Intelligence, Love, or Consciousness. Neither does eternality, universality, or immutability have any connotation of materiality. In other words, we have kept our Consciousness "stayed on God"—the Actuality—and this is what we continue to do.

In our contemplation, the word *Omniaction* appears increasingly, and it becomes more and more important. Being "full open," we accept the vital importance of this word *Omniaction*, and we hold it in contemplation, letting it reveal whatever is necessary at the moment. The omnipotent, irresistible, rhythmic, surging Omniaction which is the Universe in action will be apparent. Then the perfect activity of the planets in orbit may be realized. We are cognizant of the universal activity which we call

Omniaction. If our perception of Omniaction is great enough, we may very well sense and experience this surging, irrepressible, rhythmic activity. Inherently we know that there is no resisting—and nothing existing *to* resist—this glorious, omnipotent Omniaction.

The contemplation and experience of Omniaction inevitably brings forth in Consciousness the word *Life*. And this is a vitally important word in our contemplation. We consider the uninterrupted, omnipresent, living, loving, conscious Mind which constitutes this Universe. We contemplate the irresistible surge of this universal Essence. And we realize that this activity is Life Itself. Thus, we are aware that Life is omnipresent and omniactive.

We know that Life is Light and that Light is Life. As we sense and experience this omniactive, rhythmic surge, we are *aware* of the Life that is Light. We perceive that the Light is the Essence of all form, and we realize that the activity of the Essence is the Essence in action. Thus, we actually *see* as well as experience being the living, omniactive Life that is Light. And the peace of this experience is indescribable. Oh, it is an *active* peace. There is nothing static or inactive about it. In fact, the awareness of activity is most intense, but it is also gentle. Then we realize the gentle, living Love which is in action everywhere.

Now, our contemplation of the Universe is quite satisfying because we have actively contemplated the omniactive, living, loving, conscious Intelligence which constitutes the Universe. No doubt the word *Perfection* has also entered into our contemplation. Whether or not it has been apparent, we have inherently realized that Perfection is a universal necessity, thus, a universal fact.

In all this contemplation, we have not specifically considered the Earth planet. Yet we have known that every universal Truth we have perceived is true in and as the Earth planet. However, now it may be that we will find our attention focused upon *our* planet. If so, this is as it should be, because it means that we should be specific as well as universal in our contemplation. So we continue our contemplation, but now our attention is focused upon *this* planet. This does not mean that we consider the seeming problems of the world. Quite the contrary—we consider the world in which there are *no* problems. We do not try to change an apparently troubled world into a peaceful world. We do not try to change assumptive human beings into genuine spiritual Being. We *know* the futility of this way. We know that the earth *is* heaven when it is rightly seen. And we stand firm in our knowing.

Now, every Truth that we have seen to be a universal Truth is perceived to be true right here and now in and as this Earth planet. Thus, the Life-Consciousness-Love-Intelligence which comprises this Earth planet in Its entirety is inseparable. Conscious, living, loving, intelligent Life is indivisible right here and now. Continents, oceans, national or international assumptive boundary lines cannot separate the universal Oneness which *is* this planet.

Most important of all is the fact that the Earth planet is inseparable from the Universe Itself. The outline of our planet does not confine its Essence within its form. Neither does it exclude the Universe from its own Essence and Activity which *is* this planet. If the infinite Essence—living, conscious Intelligence—could be barred from the body of the Earth planet, God—the Universe—would have to be divided into bits and pieces of Itself. And, of course, this is impossible.

This brings us again to that most important word, *Omniaction*. We have perceived the infinite, omnipotent Universe in uninterrupted action. We have been aware of this glorious activity in, through, and as the Universe. We have experienced this perfect Omniaction in and as our own Being and Its Essence. We have realized Its inseparable nature, and we have gloried in Its intense, but peaceful, rhythmic activity. Now we can perceive this Omniaction to be omniactive in, through, and as the entire Earth planet. This being true, how could there be such terrible events as earthquakes, storms, floods, fires? There cannot actually be such destructive events. You see, there is nothing existing in or as this Universe which can act in such a terrible way. There is nothing existing in or as this Universe that can act contrary to the perfect Omniaction which is the Universe in irrepressible activity.

Omniaction *has* to act lovingly because It is Love in action. Mind, Life, Consciousness must act lovingly and perfectly because this is God—perfect, living, loving, conscious Intelligence in action. Thus, there are no evil, destructive elements in action. In fact, there are no such elements to act.

By this same token, how can there be such a thing as nuclear warfare? Is there actually a nuclear bomb, with activity and power to destroy living, conscious Mind? If this could be genuine, where would God be in all of this? Could God have absented Itself *from* Itself? No! No! No! Furthermore, what would supply such an atrocious illusion with power or activity? Mind does not act in a way that will destroy Itself. If it could act as a Self-destructive power or presence, it would not be Intelligence. Intelligence always acts intelligently, even as Love always acts lovingly.

There is no presence or power operating in, on, or as this Earth planet which is not the universal, omnipotent, intelligent Love in action. We do not *try* to bring this one and only activity into being. We know it is already existing, right here and now. Furthermore, we know that no one exists who could stop it from being what it is. This glorious, perfect, active Love exists not because of assumptive man but despite the illusion called man and all of its delusions.

We know that this world cannot really be governed by despotic little power-mad men. We know that the Mind which is Love is the *only* Intelligence and that this mind governs lovingly and intelligently. Most important of all, we know that each Identity is his own intelligent, loving governor, and his government is principled and unselfish. We do not look to assumptive man for help; neither do we fear harm from this misconception. We know that perfect government is a universal fact and that nothing can change this fact. We are aware that the *only* government is Self-government and that this is Principle governing Itself.

We know that there is no law of injustice; there is only the law of justice and Love. We know there are not many laws and that there is but one law. We know that this one law is the law of eternal, infinite, perfect, intelligent Love and that it governs infinitely as well as infinitesimally. Perhaps the ringing words of Isaiah will appear within our Consciousness:

"… and the government shall be upon his shoulder: and his name shall be called Wonderful, Counseller, The mighty God, The everlasting Father, The Prince of Peace" (Isa. 9:6).

In the Light of our illumined contemplation, these wonderful passages have a new and glorious meaning. Now we *know* what it means to say that "his name shall be called Wonderful." We know that His name is the name by which each one of us is identified. We know that His Identity is eternally established as I AM. We perceive that the I AM which is God is the only Identity in existence. Thus, the I

AM Identity is the Identity of all the peoples, the nations, and the supposed nationalities of the world. Best of all, we know that God does not oppose Itself, war against Itself, or misunderstand Itself. Thus, there can be no warring leaders, no warring nations, and no warring peoples.

Now we have arrived at the indestructibility of the eternal Body of Light. We perceive that this perfect Essence in form never came *into* existence. Neither can It go *out* of existence or be *put out* of existence. We comprehend the fact that the Body of Light really is known to be the *only* Body. *Therefore, there is no mind that knows anything about a body that can be destroyed.* It is only the deluded concept of mind which seems to imagine that the Body can be destroyed or that it has the power to destroy It. The one and *only* Mind knows nothing of destruction. Neither does this Mind know anything about a desire to punish or to destroy. Certain it is that infinite, intelligent Love has no awareness of a desire to dominate or to enslave Its own identification of Itself.

Illumined Consciousness reveals every Truth that has been stated here, and It will reveal greater and more glorious Truths as your contemplation continues. What has been presented in these pages is not a formula to be followed. Rather it is merely a presentation of the experience of numerous illumined ones when their attention, when in illumination, has been called to the Earth planet and its activity. Nevertheless, we realize that each Identity is Its own revelation and Its own revelator, and the enlightened Consciousness which you experience being must reveal Itself in Its own way.

Of one thing you can be very certain: your enlightened contemplation is powerful indeed. In fact, it is omnipotent Love in action. And it does prove its practicality in your experience, in the experience of others, and in the experience of the whole world. So it is apparent that we do not ignore the *seeming* needs of the world. Although the world appears to be immersed in turmoil, in fear, and in darkness, the everlasting Light is a constant, universal Existent. Although the seeming dream of assumptive man has turned into a nightmare, God *is* All, and God is neither a dream nor a dreamer. God, being the only One who can be identified, *has* to be the *only* Identity of you, of me, of all. So actually, there is no one who is genuinely conscious of darkness, of trouble, or of fear. It is your awareness of this Truth, my awareness of this Truth, and the awareness of everyone who is consciously enlightened that reveals It to be true here and now.

Let us no longer live on promises. Let us no longer live in the *hope* of a better world to come in the future. Let us realize that God is All—*now*. Let us perceive that God is All—*here*. It is our acceptance and full realization of this Truth that is, and must be, evidenced as the world *as it is, not as it appears to be.* We know that whatever God is, the Universe is, because God *is* the Universe. Whatever the Universe is, our Earth planet is, for God *is* the Earth planet. Whatever the Earth planet is, the Identity is, for God *is* each and every Identity.

"The people that walked in darkness have seen a great light: they that dwell in the land of the shadow of death, upon them hath the light shined" (Isa. 9:2).

Truly, here speaks enlightened Consciousness. Here is no promise of a *future* awakening. Neither does Isaiah envision a future in which Life will *become* eternal. As illumined Consciousness, Isaiah perceives that those right here and now, who seem to walk in darkness, are aware of the Light.

Yes, they are aware of more than that; they perceive that they *are* the Light right here and now. They cannot live in the "shadow of death," for they know there *is* no death. They know that Life *is* eternal and immutable. What we know, they know. What they know, we know, for we are one Consciousness, one Mind, one Life, and one Love. If we know this Truth, they *must* know it, for there is no division between us.

Truly, the undivided Light is come,
and we are the Light.

Chapter XII

The Light Is Come

Arise, shine; for thy light is come, and the glory of the Lord is risen upon thee.

—*Isa. 60:1*

Enlightened Consciousness is *your* Consciousness right here and right now. Illumined Consciousness is your *only* Consciousness. Nothing is conscious but Consciousness, and God, Consciousness, is Light. The Light is ever radiant as Its own glory—and *you are the Light.*

Illumined Consciousness cannot be attained. If It were attainable, It would be apart from your own Consciousness. It would be outside—or other than— the Consciousness you have and are. If this could be true, you would not be conscious this moment. The one universal Consciousness is not divided into separate compartments. You are not a vehicle or a receptacle into which the Light enters and from which It can depart. Neither are you a channel through which the Light flows. Because *you* live, It is radiantly alive. Indeed, the Light *is* come. It is gloriously conscious because *you* are conscious.

Beloved, behold thy Self. Dare to accept and to claim thine eternal enlightened Christ-Identity.

Dare to reject the illusion that thou art a weak, unworthy, frail mortal, abjectly pleading to *become* worthy. Is Consciousness unworthy of being conscious? Is Life unworthy to be alive? Is Mind unworthy to be intelligent? Is Love unworthy of being loving?

"Let this mind be in you, which was also in Christ Jesus: who, being in the form of God, thought it not robbery to be equal with God" (Phil. 2:5, 6). You have accepted the fact that of yourself you can do nothing, know nothing, have nothing, and be nothing. Thus, you have realized the true humility. In this humility, you have recognized the fact that only because God *is* can you be. In this same humility, you have rejected all fictitious human pride, human ambition, and human avarice. You *are* free of mortality, with all its fallacious longings, yearnings, struggles, and strife.

You are immune to the illusions of pseudo mortality. You are untouched by the illusory world of appearance. You are in the world but not of it. You are not attracted to the things of the world. Neither are you repelled by them.

> Yea, the darkness hideth not from thee; But the night shineth as the day: The darkness and the light are both alike to thee (Ps. 139:12).

Yes, the night and the day, the darkness and the Light, are both alike to you. All is Light, and there is *no* darkness. And you love—oh, *how you love.* You love because you *are* Love. You have no choice but to love. You have no choice but to be the Love you are. The Love you are is steadfast. It does not come and go. It does not ebb and flow. It loves equally everywhere, everyone, and everything. It knows nothing that is not worthy. It sees nothing that is not beautiful. The Love you are knows nothing of giving or withholding. It loves because It is perfect Love. Your Love is perfect because you are perfect Love.

Jesus said, "My kingdom is not of this world" (John 18:36). Now you too can say, "My kingdom is not of this world." Your kingdom is your Consciousness. The Consciousness you have, and are, is not concerned with an illusory world. Therefore, you are not subject to its fantasies or its fallacies. You are not subject to its assumptive laws of birth, change, and death. You are free of its illusions of sorrow, sickness, and pain. You are immune to its phantasmic laws of cause and effect. You are untouched by its delusions of cruelty, malice, greed, ambition, and avarice. Your Consciousness is not of this world; therefore, you are not moved by any appearance of sin, guilt, or self-righteousness.

Your kingdom, Consciousness, is your world. You, the enlightened One, are the king of your kingdom. You are not a ruler or a power *over* anyone or anything. You are the power of Love. You are the power of being Love. You are the power of being living, loving, conscious Intelligence. In this way only, you are the king of your kingdom. Your Consciousness is your Universe because, you see, your Universe is your Consciousness.

Who is the author of this book? *You are*— because *you* is only a word that has been used to signify the *I* that I am. If the one called "you" had not existed, this book would not have been revealed or written. Every word of Truth in this book you already know. Every Truth revealed within these pages you are.

For this reason, when you reread this book, you will say *I* wherever you find the word *you*. You will say *I am* wherever you see the words *you are*. I AM is your name. I AM is my name. I AM is the only name by which anyone can be identified.

And now, beloved, the Light *is* come and you *are* the Light. Now you can, with humility, joy, peace, and ecstasy, claim your eternal Identity in your own name: I AM.

I now claim my identity as
the Infinite, Eternal I that I am.

I am the Life that is Light. *I* am the Light that is Life, for *I* am that I AM. *I* am the Love that loves. *I* am the Intelligence that is intelligent. *I* am the Consciousness that is conscious; for *I* am that I AM. I am infinite, for *I* am Infinity. *I* am eternal, for *I* am Eternality. *I* am immutable, for *I* am Immutability. *I* am omnipresent, for *I* am Omnipresence. *I* am omniactive, for *I* am Omniaction. *I* am equally present everywhere, for *I* am *the* Everywhere.

I am the Light. *I* am the Essence of the Light. *I* am the Light in action. *I* am conscious of being the *I* that *I* am. *I* am conscious of being *only* the *I* that *I* am. *I* am the All-knowing Mind. *I* am the All-Conscious Consciousness. *I* am the All-living Life. *I* am the All-loving Love; for *I* am that I AM.

I am the All-seeing Eye. *I* am the All-hearing Ear. *I* am the All-acting Universe, for *I* am that I AM. *I* am irrepressible, living Mind. *I* am unobstructible, conscious Life. *I* am inexhaustible, living, conscious Mind, for *I* am that I AM. *I* am imperishable. *I* am indestructible. *I* am boundless, immeasurable, and indefinable. *I* am unconditioned Existence, for *I* am that I AM.

I am Truth; *I* am All that is true. *I* am Reality; *I* am All that is real. *I* am Principle; *I* am All that is principled. *I* am Life, for *I* am All that is alive. *I* am Consciousness; *I* am All that is conscious. *I* am Intelligence; *I* am All that is intelligent. *I* am Love; *I* am All that is loving, for *I* am that I AM.

I am the Perfection of All that is perfect. *I* am the Beauty of All that is beautiful. *I* am the Vision of All that sees. *I* am the Hearing of All that hears. *I* am the Experience of All that experiences. *I* am the All of All that is perfect. *I* am the All of All that is beautiful. *I* am the All of All that sees. *I* am the All of All that hears. *I* am the All of All that experiences, for *I* am that I AM.

I am the Experiencer and the Experience. *I* am the Activity and the Actor. *I* am the Knower and the Known. *I* am the Consciousness and the One who is conscious. *I* am the Impulsion and the Impelled. *I* am the Self-maintained. *I* am the Self-

217

sustained. *I* am ever new, ever whole, ever entire; *I* am Newness, Wholeness, Entirety, for *I* am that I AM.

I am beginningless, changeless, endless. *I* am birthless, ageless, deathless. *I* am pure Spirit. *I* am Soul. *I* do not come. *I* do not go. *I* remain because *I* am. *I* am the Seer and the Seen. *I* am the Be-er and the Being. *I* am the only Essence. *I* am the only activity of the Essence that *I* am. *I* am the only One who acts. *I* am the *only* Essence in action, for *I* am that I AM.

I am the universal All. *I* am the galaxies, the stars, and the planets. *I* am the suns, the moons, and the Earth planet. *I* am the ocean, the tide, the wave, and the drop of water. *I* am the beach and every grain of sand. *I* am the mountain and the valley. *I* am the rose and the thistle. *I* am the desert and the forest. *I* am the field, the harvest, and the harvester; for *I* am that I AM.

I am the bird and its song. *I* am the tree, its blossom and its fruit. *I* am the vine and the husbandman. *I* am the seed, the root, and the fruit of the vine. *I* am the snow, the rain, and the green living grass. *I* am the perfume of the flower. *I* am the sighing of the wind in the forest. *I* am the roar of the ocean. *I* am the soft cooing of the dove. *I* am the universal Symphony. *I* am the Music of the Spheres, for *I* am that I AM.

I am indivisible. *I* am inseparable. *I* am timeless, spaceless. *I* am unconditioned. *I* am free. *I* am invulnerable. *I* am immune to all illusions of phantasmic mortality. *I* am the only One who knows. *I* am All that is known. *I* know only that which *I* am, for *I* am that I AM. *I* am the Inspiration and the inspired One. *I* am the Revelation and the Revelator. *I* am a Movement and a Rest. *I* rest in action. *I* am unlabored, effortless Omniaction, for *I* am that I AM.

I am fetterless. *I* am weightless. *I* am immune to any assumed law of gravity. *I* am free of suppositional density. *I* know nothing of solidity. *I* know nothing of restrictions or limitations. *I* am free of all assumptive bondage to person, place, or thing, for *I* am impersonal, infinite, conscious Love. *I* am free of all fruitless planning, scheming, or thought-taking, for *I* am Consciousness, and *I* am conscious now. *I* know nothing of cause and effect, for *I* am that I AM.

I am all Existence. *I* am the Here and the Now of All that exists. *I* am Completeness. *I* am Supply. *I* am the Completeness that comprises the Supply *I* am. *I* am Self-governed. *I* am the Universal Order. *I* am omnipresent, omniactive, living, loving, conscious Intelligence. *I* am the surging, orderly, rhythmic Omniaction in ceaseless, effortless movement. *I* am the Universal Activity, and *I* am the Universe that acts, for *I* am that I AM.

I am the Beauty and that which is beautiful. *I* am the Perfection and that which is perfect. *I* am the Completeness and that which is complete. *I* am the Radiance and that which is radiant. *I* am the Light and that which is alight.

The Light *I* am is never interrupted. The Light *I* am can never dim. The Light *I* am does not falter. The Light *I* am does not tarry.

I am the Light, for I am that I AM. Truly the Light is come, and I am the Light.

About the Author

During early childhood, Marie S. Watts began questioning: "Why am I? What am I? Where is God? What is God?"

After experiencing her first illumination at seven years of age, her hunger for the answers to these questions became intensified. Although she became a concert pianist, her search for the answers continued, leading her to study all religions, including those of the East.

Finally, ill and unsatisfied, she gave up her profession of music, discarded all books of ancient and modern religions, kept only the Bible, and went into virtual seclusion from the world for some eight years. It was out of the revelations and illuminations she experienced during those years, revelations that were sometimes the very opposite of what she had hitherto believed, that her own healing was realized and that her book *The Ultimate* came.

During all the previous years she had been active in helping others. After *The Ultimate* was published, she devoted herself exclusively to the continuance of the healing work and to lecturing and teaching.

Revelations continued to come to her from within her own consciousness, and they were set forth as she did in this book.

To all seekers for Light, for Truth, for God, for an understanding of their own true Being, this book will serve as a revolutionary but wholly satisfying guide.

Made in the USA
Coppell, TX
02 September 2022

82496091R00132